D1365082

TWENTIETH CENTURY INTERPRETATIONS

OF

A PORTRAIT OF THE ARTIST AS A YOUNG MAN

A Collection of Critical Essays

Edited by
WILLIAM M. SCHUTTE

Prentice-Hall, Inc. *Englewood Cliffs, N. J.*

A Note on the Form

The authors of the essays in this volume used several different editions of *A Portrait of the Artist as a Young Man* some of which are not now readily available. In order to increase the usefulness of this volume, all page references to the *Portrait* have been converted so as to refer to the standard edition published in 1964 by The Viking Press, Inc. (Compass Books): no symbol precedes page references to the *Portrait*.

Page references to other works by Joyce are preceded by an appropriate symbol and, where necessary, have been converted so as to refer to the following editions:

SH—*Stephen Hero,* ed. John J. Slocum and Herbert Cahoon. Norfolk, Conn.: New Directions Pub. Corp., 1963.

U—*Ulysses*. New York: Random House, Inc., Modern Library Edition, 1942, etc. and New York: Random House, Inc., Modern Library Edition (Revised), 1961. Reference is made to both editions: the page of the earlier edition before the slash mark; that page of the more recent edition after it.

F—*Finnegans Wake*. New York: The Viking Press, Inc., 1945.

CW—*The Critical Writings of James Joyce,* ed. Ellsworth Mason and Richard Ellmann. New York: The Viking Press, Inc., 1959.

Current printing (last number):

10 9 8 7 6 5 4 3 2 1

Prentice-Hall International, Inc. (*London*)

809
JOYCE

Contents

Introduction

by *William M. Schutte*

Joyce's *A Portrait of the Artist as a Young Man* has been with us now for more than half a century. For much of that time its importance as a work of art has been generally accepted and its wide influence has been recognized. Among novelists it has inspired countless imitations and variants, acknowledged and unacknowledged; among scholars and critics it has generated hundreds of articles and not a few books. Today it is almost certainly the most widely read novel in university literature courses, and it has begun to make its way in secondary school honors sections. It has been presented over the radio and portions of it are available on records. At least two dramatizations have received professional production. Still the *Portrait* remains an enigma: it continues to thwart our best efforts to define it.

As we gain a better understanding of certain of its elements—its symbols, its sources, its Dublin setting, its relation to Joyce's life, its mythological content—the problem of definition becomes paradoxically more difficult and more challenging. The essays that follow are among the most perceptive that have been written in the past twenty years. Each explores a different facet of Joyce's book and together they provide a variety of approaches to it. This introduction may suggest others. But in the end each reader must weigh the evidence and reach his own conclusions, for the *Portrait*, although its form may be less complex, is no more susceptible to final definition than *Ulysses* or *Finnegans Wake*.

I

On February 2, 1882, when Joyce was born in Rathgar, a residential suburb of Dublin, Ireland was a stagnating backwater. For centuries she had been suppressed, exploited, and forbidden to develop any product which might compete with English goods. Only thirty years before, the great potato famine had destroyed a million and a half Irishmen and forced another million to emigrate. Fifteen years had passed since the most recent attempt to secure Irish rights by armed revolt against British rule; like so many others, it had collapsed in an inglorious tangle of betrayal and ineptitude. Few thoughtful people could have denied the cogency of the argument put forward by Stephen Dedalus in the *Portrait* when responding to an invitation to join the Nationalist cause: "No honourable and sincere man . . . has given up to you his life and his youth and his affections from the days of Tone to those of Parnell but you sold him to the enemy or failed him in need or reviled him and left him for another. . . . Ireland is the old sow that eats her farrow." (203) Despite the concessions which from time to time Charles Stewart Parnell had been able to secure from the Parliament in London, Ireland in 1882 was drab, impoverished, divided by factional disputes. The natural beauty of the landscape served only to remind Irishmen how badly off they were.

The home into which Joyce was born was more than comfortable. As a young man John Stanislaus Joyce had fallen heir to a portion of the little wealth there was in Ireland for Irishmen. A man of great wit, talent, and charm, he was a well-known and popular figure in Dublin. One quality, however, he had been denied: the ability to hang on to money. Two months before James's birth he had dissipated the last of the funds inherited from his father and had taken the first step in the direction of bankruptcy by mortgaging one of his properties. In a dozen years there would be no money left with which to feed the ten children his wife, the former Mary Jane Murray, had borne him. And there would be no prospect of recovery, for John Stanislaus was temperamentally unsuited to earning a steady living.

The eldest of the ten children, James had a brief glimpse of a world of servants and nurseries, chandeliers and pier glasses, smoking platters and blazing puddings. From his sixth to his ninth year he was sent to an exclusive Jesuit boarding school, Clongowes Wood, in the rolling country west of Dublin. But in June 1891 his father lost his position as Collector of Rates in Dublin and decided that he could no longer afford to keep his son in Clongowes. This decision marked a significant phase in the family's gradual but uninterrupted descent into the inferno of Dublin poverty. Throughout his school years Joyce was a victim of his family's failing fortunes, and he never forgot the degradation and shame in which his family's position involved him.

Through the intervention of the former rector of Clongowes, who recalled his ability as a student, Joyce began his secondary education as a "free boy" at the Jesuit-run Belvedere College in 1893. Five years later he moved on to University College, the small Catholic university on Stephen's Green, which shared with the more distinguished, Protestant-controlled Trinity College the responsibility for higher education in Dublin. At both institutions Joyce found excellent teachers and stimulating companions from whom, no doubt, he learned much that was useful to him later. But he was an erratic performer who followed the prescribed curriculum only as it suited his interests and inclinations. Much of his real education was derived from his ceaseless exploration of the Dublin streets, his extensive reading in contemporary literature, and his investigation of obscure volumes to be found in the National Library, Marsh's Library, or the bookstalls along the Liffey. At the University he made a reputation by reading a provocative paper on "Drama and Life" before the Literary and Historical Society, by attacking in a privately printed pamphlet the new Irish Literary Theatre founded by Yeats and Lady Gregory, and especially by publishing an article on Ibsen in the *Fortnightly Review,* perhaps the leading English literary journal of the time.

All this time Joyce was living at home, moving with his family through a series of temporary residences, each shabbier and dirtier than the last. He was given no opportunity to forget that his family was settling into the morass of filth and hunger and misery which for centuries had robbed the country of its energy and its creativity. Close as he felt to his family—and in his attitude toward them at least Joyce must be distinguished from his fictional counterpart, Stephen Dedalus— he finally determined that his only salvation was to leave behind the deadening atmosphere of his homeland and seek his freedom and his fortune on the Continent.

As it happened, he had to escape twice. A few months of bohemian existence in Paris ended abruptly in April 1903 with the arrival of a telegram "MOTHER DYING COME HOME FATHER." Mary Jane Joyce did not in fact die until August. For more than a year after her death Joyce remained in Ireland, maintaining himself haphazardly by borrowing, sponging on friends, writing articles, and even teaching school for a while. More important, he published an occasional poem, wrote short stories, and began a novel (*Stephen Hero*). But as time passed, he became more and more restive in Dublin. Eventually he determined to leave. In October 1904 he sailed off with Nora Barnacle, a Galway girl whom he had met in Dublin, to make his way as a Berlitz instructor on the Continent.

Thereafter Joyce saw Ireland only on a few brief visits, the last in 1912. Until the First World War he lived and taught in Italy; during the war he stayed as a neutral in Switzerland; between the wars his home was Paris. In all this time Joyce was busy writing, traveling, drinking, quarreling, and talking. But there were no great events. He and Nora had two children: Georgio, born in 1905; and Lucia, born two years later. From 1917 onward he was plagued by diseases of the eye which ultimately required eleven operations, and during the last decade of his life he suffered great anguish through the mental illness of his daughter.

Meanwhile his early books were refused by publishers, and *Ulysses,* issued at Paris in 1922, was banned by censors in England and the

United States. With the publication of this work, however, Joyce's reputation was secured. The brash young man of considerable promise but no accomplishment who left Dublin in 1904 with nothing became in the Twenties one of the world's most prominent men of letters, surrounded by disciples and deferred to by his peers. Fragments of his *Work in Progress* were released from time to time during the Twenties and Thirties. They were awaited with eager anticipation by the literary world, and a defense and critical analysis of the first fragments appeared a decade before the completed work was published as *Finnegans Wake* in 1939.[1] Two years later Joyce has gone. He died in Zürich on January 13, 1941, after an operation for a perforated duodenal ulcer.

In the forty years that had passed since the appearance of his article on Ibsen in the *Fortnightly Review,* Joyce had published (other than a few ephemeral pieces) two slim volumes of poetry, a play, a collection of short stories, and three novels. Not a large output for a major writer. But Joyce had one asset denied to all but the very greatest artists: the ability to move forward in each of his works without repeating himself and to make each advance both an inimitable performance and a landmark in the history of his art. Leaving aside his poems and his play—which are derivative—critics have long recognized that each volume represented a unique contribution to the art of fiction. No modern writer has been able to match this achievement, and none has so profoundly influenced the shape of modern fiction.

The sturdy, compact short stories of *Dubliners,* although no doubt they owe much to Chekhov, Maupassant, Flaubert, and perhaps other writers as well, are nonetheless unique and have been credited with setting the norm for the modern, sophisticated short story. *Ulysses,* as everyone knows, is "*the* stream-of-consciousness novel." It is, of course, a great deal more: a "chaffering, allincluding, most farraginous chronicle," as Joyce himself called it (*U,* 416/423). It is an attempt at an inclusive portrait of the modern world, making use of every device in the novelist's bag and some especially invented for the occasion. Its superbly conducted orchestration of the infinite detail of human civilization is intended to reveal to us the essence of the confused present in which we live. And finally there is the vast hulk of *Finnegans Wake.* Is it, as its partisans claim, Joyce's masterpiece? Or is it in the last analysis "an artistic failure"?[2] So far there is no agreement among critics. But few will deny that in this work Joyce has pushed both language and the novel form through the boundaries previously set for them. The novel will not be the same again.

---

[1] It was called *Our Exagmination round His Factification for Incamination of Work in Progress* (Paris, 1929), contained essays by twelve of Joyce's friends, and was approved by Joyce himself.

[2] S. L. Goldberg, *James Joyce* (Edinburgh and London, 1962), p. 103.

II

Between *Dubliners* and *Ulysses* in the Joyce canon we find *A Portrait of the Artist as a Young Man,* which was completed in 1915. It made its unique contribution, on which Joyce and others later built, by showing how the novel could be given added power through a new concentration of vision.

At the end of *A Portrait of the Artist as a Young Man* Joyce placed the words: "Dublin 1904. Trieste 1914." The dates do not refer, as one might suppose, to the composition of the text to which they were appended. Instead they enclose the ten years between the initial impulse to write an account of an artist's youth and the beginning of serial publication of the final text in the English journal *The Egoist* on February 2, 1914, Joyce's thirty-second birthday. During those ten years the account took three distinct forms.

The first—called "A Portrait of the Artist" at the suggestion of Joyce's brother Stanislaus—was the badly overwritten production of a day, a curious melange of essay and narrative in which the young writer presented himself in what was to become the characteristic stance of Joyce and his alter egos: as the embattled but ever-defiant Artist, the stag with "flashing antlers" harried relentlessly by the powers that rule the world. The tone, like the content, fluctuates: at one moment the reader seems called upon to identify with the gallant young man and applaud his youthful idealism; in the next he is clearly asked to consider this idealism with ironic detachment. The result, even when viewed from the perspective of Joyce's later accomplishments, is confused and unsatisfactory. It is promising undergraduate writing at its most extravagant, full of undigested notions and purple passages, at the opposite extreme from the carefully controlled spareness of the short stories which Joyce was soon to write at George Russell's request for the *Irish Homestead.* These were the stories published in 1914, with some additions and after protracted negotiations, as *Dubliners.*

Early in 1904 Joyce submitted his essay-narrative to the Dublin literary review *Dana.* It was rejected. "I can't print what I can't understand," said the editor, John Eglinton. Joyce's reaction was prompt. Within a month he was well along in planning an autobiographical novel, to be called *Stephen Hero,* into which he packed incident after thinly disguised incident from his own life.

In this endeavor he may have been encouraged by the posthumous appearance during the preceding year of Samuel Butler's *The Way of All Flesh* (written between 1873 and 1885), the chronicle of another young artist's growth and of his revolt against the prescriptions of the social order. But he was no doubt influenced, too, by the autobiographical works of authors he greatly admired: Augustine's *Confessions,* Goethe's *Werther* and *Wilhelm Meister,* and Newman's *Apologia pro*

Vita Sua. Since he felt himself not unworthy of their company,[3] it is not surprising that he chose to follow in their steps.

So for the next three years he labored over *Stephen Hero.* A generous portion of the manuscript has survived, enough to suggest that it is indeed the apprentice work of a genuine artist. Individual incidents are treated with the skill that one might expect from the author of *Dubliners.* Some of the characters are presented with striking clarity. But the author is much too close to his material. He cannot reject the peripheral, and he cannot resist the editorial. He cannot yet give his work artistic shape and final meaning.

By the time Joyce had reached the university phase of Stephen Hero's life, he had written 24 of a projected 63 chapters and had filled well over a thousand pages of manuscript. And although he wrote to his brother on February 28, 1905, "It would be easy for me to do short novels if I chose but what I want to wear away in this novel cannot be worn away except by constant dropping," [4] he seems ultimately to have concluded that the artist may achieve his ends with more efficient methods. By September 1907 he had abandoned the massive effort to wear his readers down and had selected what was to be the final form for his novel: five brief chapters containing incidents largely drawn from *Stephen Hero* but refocussed so that each incident and each detail would contribute significantly to his theme, the development of the young artist. By April 7, 1908, he had written the first three chapters; then, finding it impossible to continue, he put the work aside for six years. When Dora Marsden, through the intervention of Ezra Pound, agreed to publish it in *The Egoist,* Joyce had one of his bursts of creative energy. Although Richard Ellmann believes that the final chapters were probably incomplete when the first began to appear, the last pages reached Pound in London during August of 1915.

The two early versions, one complete and the other a fragment, provide the scholar with valuable material for his analysis of the creative process. Both versions, however, were rejected by Joyce, and they should not be permitted to distract us from the *Portrait* itself, which is, as Joyce thought it, an artistic unity for which the others are only preliminary sketches. The early narrative-essay is at best an unstructured and sometimes incoherent sketch; and Joyce himself passed judgment on *Stephen Hero*: "What rubbish it is!" he wrote to Harriet Weaver in 1934. No doubt he was harsh in evaluating his rough draft, for *Stephen Hero* has its intermittent virtues. Clearly, however, he had no intention of publishing it, and in 1911 he would have burned the manuscript had not his sister rescued it from the fire.

We should be wary, too, of considering the *Portrait* merely a prelude

[3] See, for example, his letter to Ibsen in Richard Ellmann, *James Joyce* (New York, 1959), pp. 89–91.
[4] Ellmann, p. 200.

to its more complex successor, *Ulysses.* It is not. Stephen Dedalus is a major figure in *Ulysses,* the two books share a number of other characters, and some details of the later book can be explained only by reference to the *Portrait* and *Dubliners.* But each of Joyce's published works was intended to stand by itself, and each has proved perfectly capable of doing so. *Ulysses* is unquestionably far more ambitious in what it attempts and in the techniques it uses. On the other hand, there is much to be said for John V. Kelleher's conclusion that "the *Portrait* is Joyce's one perfected work, evenly sustained and controlled from end to end by a talent in calm dominion over its theme, its instruments, and itself." [5]

"Perfected" is not a word that was used when the *Portrait* first appeared as a book in 1916–1917. Many reviewers recognized signs of mastery and even of genius, but most saw it as seriously flawed either by what seemed prurient realism, or by onesidedness in presenting Stephen's world, or by lack of organization, or by the intrusion of undramatic and irrelevant sermons and discussions of esthetics.[6] Looking back on their struggles to come to terms with the book, we now can recognize that their difficulties were caused by the appearance of a new type of novel, to which they could apply standards suitable only for evaluating the type to which they had long been accustomed. (Joyce handed them the same problem with the even more formidable novelties of *Ulysses* and *Finnegans Wake.*) It has taken us a half century and a very large amount of criticism to come to a somewhat clearer understanding of Joyce's book and its divergences from the conventional novel.

Part of the difficulty stems from Joyce's frequent and brilliant use of the standard tools of the old form. Indeed, his early reviewers tended to attribute the presence of passages which offended "good taste" to an obsession with "a brilliant and nasty variety of pseudo-realism." [7] Realism there certainly is in the *Portrait*—in the famous Christmas Dinner scene and in the University College scenes, for example—but the vivid and detailed presentation of episodes from Stephen's life constitutes but one of many methods used by Joyce in outlining the development of his young artist. Here, as in his later and more ambitious works, he refuses to construct his novel on the basis of any previously recognized program. He can no more be called a realist than an impressionist, symbolist, associationist, or psychological novelist. Rather he uses a variety of techniques, each of which has its own function in the plan for the book as a whole.

[5] "The Perceptions of Joyce," *Atlantic Monthly,* CCI (March, 1958), p. 88.

[6] For an extensive survey of the early reviews, see Marvin Magalaner and Richard M. Kain, *Joyce: The Man, The Work, The Reputation* (New York, 1956), p. 102.

[7] *Weekly Times* (Manchester), March 3, 1917. Quoted in Magalaner and Kain, p. 102.

III

What then does the *Portrait* do? How are we to define this book which seems so uncomplicated when placed beside *Ulysses* and *Finnegans Wake* but which has proved so difficult to pin down? It calls itself a portrait of the artist as a young man; its theme is the development of the artist from that point in his early childhood when he first becomes conscious of the world's attempt to assert dominion over his life to the last day of his young manhood, the day before he sets off in pursuit of the goal which in the course of the book he has identified and apprehended.

Characteristically even the title provides problems. Through Frank Budgen, Joyce himself has warned us not to forget its last four words, as some of his early critics did.[8] Fair enough. But the problems go beyond that. We are not to be given the portrait of *an* artist as a young man but of *the* artist. How are we to understand "the artist"? Is Joyce writing autobiography or is he writing about the type of the artist? A comment to Budgen suggests the former: "I haven't let this young man off very lightly, have I? Many writers have written about themselves. I wonder if any one of them has been as candid as I have?" [9] And we recall that the phrase "portrait of the artist" is traditionally given to *self*-portraits.

Is this book a self-portrait, then? Some of the early reviewers and admirers thought so. Many of its incidents closely parallel incidents in Joyce's life. What is more, Joyce's schoolfellows at Clongowes Wood school became Stephen's schoolfellows at Clongowes Wood under their real names; men still walking Dublin's streets also walked through the *Portrait* bearing their own names; and numerous well-known Dublin figures, including Joyce's mother and father and some of his university friends, were immediately recognizable beneath their pseudonyms. Small wonder that the early reviewers saw the book as thinly disguised autobiography.

Today, however, we have good evidence from Joyce's brother Stanislaus and from his Dublin contemporaries that numerous details and even major incidents of the *Portrait* are not based on events in Joyce's life but on events in the lives of those around him. J. F. Byrne, the model for Cranly, has stated that it was he, not Joyce, who discussed with the Dean of Studies the art of lighting fires.[10] David Sheehy has pointed out that Joyce *did* take off the rector of Belvedere in a school play; though Stephen is urged to do so, he

---

[8] *James Joyce and The Making of "Ulysses"* (Bloomington: Indiana University Press, 1960), p. 60.

[9] Budgen, p. 51.

[10] *Silent Years: An Autobiography with Memoirs of James Joyce and Our Ireland* (New York, 1953), pp. 33–35.

does not.[11] As a source of information about Joyce's life, therefore, the *Portrait* is only partially reliable. One may wonder if the same may be said of its reliability as a source of information about Joyce's thinking.

In recent years we have learned that to ask whether the *Portrait* is autobiographical is to ask the wrong question. For Stephen both is and is not the young Joyce. James Joyce both is and is not the Artist as a young man. The evidence of Joyce's practice suggests that he shared the view expressed by Stephen in his discourse on the forms of art:

> The personality of the artist, at first a cry or a cadence or a mood and then a fluid and lambent narrative, finally refines itself out of existence, impersonalizes itself, so to speak. The esthetic image in the dramatic form is life purified in and reprojected from the human imagination. (215)

Stephen is the young Joyce "purified in and reprojected from the human imagination" of the mature artist, who must, in Stephen's words, "try slowly and humbly and constantly to express, to press out again, from the gross earth or what it brings forth, from sound and shape and colour which are the prison gates of our soul, an image of the beauty we have come to understand." (207) This is what Joyce attempted to do with the only gross matter he found suitable for the purpose, his own life as a potential artist. The flawed, "impure" young Joyce is the raw material from which Stephen Dedalus is created; his experience is the raw material for Stephen's life. But both the life and the experience must be refined and their imperfections removed before they can take their proper place in a work of art. In this book, therefore, Joyce uses his own life as a framework for the novel but feels perfectly free to revise his biography for the purposes of art or to import into it any details or incidents which will help him to reveal the evolution of the Artist as a Young Man.

The methods Joyce used to demonstrate this evolution were novel, and to many shocking. The failure of *Stephen Hero,* in which he had attempted to overwhelm the reader by sheer weight of what he thought to be significant incident, led Joyce to an opposite technique. But the *Portrait,* as finally conceived, is more than a mere selection of highlights from the earlier effort. Even those incidents which he retained are drastically rewritten to serve new ends.

In his revision Joyce sought not only to eliminate every detail which did not contribute actively to his portrait, but also to endow those details which remained with multiple significance. A conscientious reader of contemporary literature, he was aware of and adopted techniques exploited by the Continental symbolist writers. The structure of the *Portrait* with its interweaving of themes, symbols and

[11] *May It Please the Court* (Dublin, 1951), p. 8.

motifs more closely resembles the structure of a poem than of a traditional novel. "Plot" is internalized. Not Dublin or Ireland, but
Stephen's consciousness is "the stage on which the dramatic action
unfolds." [12] The plot of the book is Stephen's struggle for independence, as a potential Artist, against a formidable battery of opponents
who demand his allegiance:

> The constant voices of his father and of his masters, urging him to be
> a gentleman above all things and urging him to be a good Catholic
> above all things . . . another voice urging him to be strong and manly
> and healthy and . . . another voice . . . to be true to his country and
> help to raise up her fallen language and tradition. In the profane world
> . . . a worldly voice would bid him raise up his father's fallen state by
> his labours, and, meanwhile, the voice of his school comrades urged him
> to be a decent fellow, to shield others from blame or beg them off and
> to do his best to get free days for the school. (83–84)

Hugh Kenner has suggested that the *Portrait* opens "amid elaborate counterpoint. The first two pages . . . enact the entire action
in microcosm." [13] They are a prelude. And if they do not enact the
entire action, at least in them one finds hints of the significant problems that preoccupy Stephen Dedalus, the Artist as a young man, as
he reaches toward maturity: sin and retribution, paternity (divine and
consubstantial) and maternity, the tyranny of the social order, the
artist's relation to his material. With each the young artist must come
to terms before the *Portrait* is concluded. In the sections which follow,
the seeds planted here grow, each in its turn, to dominate the landscape of the book as Stephen moves from grammar school to secondary
school and finally to the university.

Joyce's method is everywhere indirect. Gone is the explicit commentary of *Stephen Hero* ("This young man thought. . . ."). Instead
Joyce uses a variety of methods to suggest, to imply, and ultimately
to control the reader's reaction to his material. The most important
are symbol, motif and style.

IV

Much has been written about the role of symbol and motif in the
Portrait. Barbara Seward, for example, has demonstrated how the rose,
with its multiple associations in Western culture, contributes at many
points to the development of its major themes. Others have studied
the use of Dedalus and Icarus, John the Baptist, the God Thoth, the

[12] Robert D. Ryf, *A New Approach to Joyce: The Portrait as a Guidebook* (Berke-
ley and Los Angeles: University of California Press, 1964), p. 57.
[13] *Dublin's Joyce* (London, 1955), p. 114.

eucharist, the bat, water, and numerous other figures. Recently Lee
Lemon has made a useful distinction between the symbol, which
brings meaning to the novel from outside, and the motif, which ac-
quires meaning through its use in the novel. Lemon has examined
Joyce's use of such important motifs as hands and eyes and has argued
that the *Portrait* "is the first novel in which motifs *per se* are of primary importance, the first novel in which both theme and structure
depend upon such minor elements." [14]

Certainly the more one reads in Joyce's text, the more one is impressed by both the subtley and the pervasiveness of his use of motif
and symbol. The most innocent of sentences becomes charged with
meaning as one sees it in the context of related elements. When, for
example, we first read on the second page of the text that "the evening
air was pale and chilly and after every charge and thud of the foot-
ballers the greasy leather orb flew like a heavy bird through the grey
light," we may recognize simply an effective descriptive sentence. Only
when we read the final phrases in the light of the many other references to flying birds and flying men, when we recognize that the word
"greasy" takes on particularly unsavory connotations as the novel pro-
gresses (see especially pp. 111 and 174), and when we discover that
"chilly" is the first in a subtly insinuated series of references to heat
and cold which gradually prepare us for the knowledge that Stephen
is coming down with influenza—only when we recall all of these
matters do we grasp the full import of this innocent-seeming bit of
descriptive prose.

Joyce seldom calls attention to such details. But each contributes to
the ultimate impact of the novel on its readers. Even less obtrusive and
equally important is the *Portrait*'s style, to which critics have given
far less of their time than to its symbols.

To understand the function of the book's style we must return to
a consideration of what Joyce seems to have been attempting as he
recast *Stephen Hero*. A most provocative hint comes, curiously enough,
from the opening paragraph of the early sketch which was rejected
by *Dana*:

> The features of infancy are not commonly reproduced in the ado-
> lescent portrait for, so capricious are we, that we cannot or will not
> conceive the past in any other than its iron memorial aspect. Yet the
> past assuredly implies a fluid succession of presents, the development of
> an entity of which our actual present is a phase only. Our world, again,
> recognises its acquaintance chiefly by the characters of beard and inches
> and is, for the most part, estranged from those of its members who
> seek through some art, by some process of the mind as yet untabulated,
> to liberate from the personalized lumps of matter that which is their
> individuating rhythm, the first or formal relation of their parts. But for

[14] See this volume, p. 42.

such as these a portrait is not an identificative paper but rather the curve of an emotion.[15]

In *A Portrait of the Artist* Joyce finally was able to carry through successfully the program which he had outlined in 1904. One suspects that he abandoned *Stephen Hero* because despite his best efforts the past was there falling into an "iron memorial aspect." He had not yet found the technique he needed to capture the "individuating rhythm" of that "fluid succession of presents" which constitutes the past. In the *Portrait,* using nineteen presents grouped into five chapters, he seems to have done so to his own satisfaction.

The technique which Joyce developed is designed to reveal, not merely to record, the essential nature of each of the nineteen presents as it impinges on the consciousness of Stephen Dedalus. As an artist, Joyce wishes to share with his reader not only *what* Stephen apprehends at any one point in his career, but also *how* he apprehends. For this purpose the indispensable agent is style. As the action moves from present to present in the chronological progress of the potential Artist toward maturity, the style subtly modulates to reflect inevitable changes in the quality of Stephen's apprehension of the world about him. In a very real sense, the style of any one section *is* Stephen at a particular point in time. And the styles of the sections taken together constitute the individuating rhythm which is Joyce's portrait of the Artist as a young man.

We should remind ourselves, however, that only in brief snatches does Joyce attempt to suggest the unselected stream of Stephen's consciousness: "Did anyone ever hear such drivel? Lord Almighty! Who ever heard of ivy whining on a wall?" (179) More often he uses the traditional third person summary account: "The names of articles of dress worn by women or of certain soft and delicate stuffs used in their making brought always to his mind a delicate and sinful perfume. As a boy he had imagined. . . ." (155) But in much of the book he uses a combination of the two: "Eleven! Then he was late for that lecture too. What day of the week was it? He stopped at a newsagent's to read the headline of a placard. Thursday. Ten to eleven, English; eleven to twelve, French; twelve to one, physics. He fancied to himself the English lecture and felt, even at that distance, restless and helpless. He saw the heads of his classmates. . . ." (177)

---

[15] Robert Scholes and Richard M. Kain, *The Workshop of Daedalus: James Joyce and the Raw Materials for "A Portrait of the Artist as a Young Man"* (Evanston, 1965), p. 60. Reprinted by permission of the Estate of James Joyce. Cf. also Joyce's definition of *rhythm* in his Paris Notebook: "Rhythm seems to be the first or formal relation of part to part in any whole or of a whole to its part or parts, or of any part to the whole of which it is a part. . . . Parts constitute a whole as far as they have a common end." (*Ibid.,* p. 54). In the *Portrait* Stephen defines rhythm in almost the same words. (206)

Nonetheless, as F. Parvin Sharpless points out, in the *Portrait* everything that occurs is presented through "the exclusive subjectivity of the protagonist, a subjectivity, moreover, which itself is in motion through time in a way that requires it to reflect even its subjectivity differently from one moment to the next." [16] To achieve this end Joyce uses an infinite variety of subtle stylistic variations. The elementary vocabulary, lack of punctuation, and simple, associative sentences of the very first section reflect the mode of apprehension characteristic of a small but sensitive child: "When you wet the bed first it is warm then it gets cold. His mother put on the oilsheet. It had a queer smell. His mother had a nicer smell than his father. She played on the piano the sailor's hornpipe for him to dance." In sharp contrast are the fragmented diary entries of the last pages. Ranging as they do between the detached sardonic and the committed ecstatic they project the present of the young Artist about to take flight and leave behind him the nets in which his world has tried and failed to hold his spirit. Between these extremes are seventeen sections, each with its individuating movement and style. In the second section of the first chapter, for example, the style reflects the confusion and tentativeness of the small boy surrounded by a large world he has only begun to understand:

> What was the right answer to the question? He had given two and still Wells laughed. But Wells must know the right answer for he was in third of grammar. He tried to think of Wells's mother but he did not dare to raise his eyes to Wells's face. He did not like Wells's face. It was Wells who had shouldered him into the square ditch the day before because he would not swop his little snuffbox for Wells's seasoned hacking chestnut, the conqueror of forty. (14)

The vague, nineteenth-century romanticism which gives birth to Stephen's dream of Mercedes is reflected in the language of the passage describing it: "The peace of the gardens and the kindly lights in the windows poured a tender influence into his restless heart." (64) When, later on, Stephen is in the throes of lust, the rhythm is sinuous and decadent: "He felt some dark presence moving irresistibly upon him from the darkness, a presence subtle and murmurous as a flood filling him wholly with itself. Its murmur beseiged his ears like the murmur of some multitude in sleep; its subtle streams penetrated his being." (100) When he repents and takes on piety, the prose becomes flat, analytical, almost businesslike:

> His daily life was laid out in devotional areas. By means of ejaculations and prayers he stored up ungrudgingly for the souls in purgatory centuries of days and quarantines and years; yet the spiritual triumph which

[16] See this volume, p. 97.

he felt in achieving with ease so many fabulous ages of canonical penances did not wholly reward his zeal of prayer since he could never
know how much temporal punishment he had remitted by way of suffrage
for the agonized souls: and fearful lest in the midst of the purgatorial
fire, which differed from the infernal only in that it was not everlasting,
his penance might avail no more than a drop of moisture, he drove his
soul daily through an increasing circle of works of supererogation. (147)

In the remaining pages the style continues to define the stages of
Stephen's development. Among others we hear the vague, exalted,
almost hysterical lyricism of the passage describing his discovery of
his vocation; the workaday prose in which is recorded his intellectual
revolt; and the "luxurious language" (181) derived from Pater and
the *fin de siècle* decadents in which his unfettered imagination bathes
as he writes his poem.

A Portrait of the Artist provides us, then, with a series of nineteen
vignettes from the life of the Artist as a young man. Each has its characteristic style which reflects, with appropriate variations to accom-
modate changes of mood or situation and with far more subtlety than
this summary account has indicated, the rhythms of one significant
stage in Stephen's development. The *Portrait,* like *Ulysses* and *Finnegans Wake,* has no one style. What makes it a distinctive landmark
in modern literature—and what contributed most to the confusion of
its early readers—is the comprehensive way in which its style reflects
the developing consciousness of the artist-hero.

V

Although some knowledge of how symbol, motif, and style cooperate
to give meaning to the events of the narrative is essential if one is to
read the *Portrait* as Joyce wished it to be read, such knowledge is
only the beginning of understanding. In the pages which follow are
studies of other aspects of the book, including S. L. Goldberg's comprehensive analysis of the function of Stephen's long lecture on esthetic theory and recent comment by Wayne Booth and F. Parvin
Sharpless on the vexed question of esthetic distance, over which critics
have been arguing ever since Hugh Kenner insisted that Joyce had
given us a portrait of a prig. These and other arguments will no
doubt continue. The richness, the intricacy, and the continuing fascination of the *Portrait,* particularly for those younger readers who find
in Stephen's struggles and sufferings the material of their own lives,
have earned it an assured place in our literature.

PART ONE

Interpretations

A Portrait of the Artist as a Young Man

by J. I. M. Stewart

A Portrait of the Artist as a Young Man, essentially the story of Joyce's own break with the Catholic Church and discovery of his true vocation, was published in 1916, at the end of a process of gestation covering many years. Joyce had begun an autobiographical novel while still in his teens, and he persevered with it until it was 150,000 words long and could be regarded as approximately half finished. About 1908 he decided to rewrite the book on a smaller scale and different method, and it appears probable that the greater part of the original manuscript was then destroyed. The only considerable fragment certainly preserved, which has been published under Joyce's original title of *Stephen Hero*, is rather longer than the whole perfected work but corresponds only to the final third of it. The technique of *Stephen Hero* is objective, explicit and ploddingly documentary. It is the only one of Joyce's works self-evidently and at once to rebut Wyndham Lewis's charge that here is a writer stimulated only by ways of doing things, and not by things to be done. It thus has some claim to be considered as a substantive work, with an illuminating place in the development of Joyce's writing, and it certainly possesses the curious interest of closely defining the whole basic structure of Joyce's personality. Nevertheless the mature *Portrait* is of altogether superior artistic significance. Its opening sentence exhibits the new technique:

> ONCE upon a time and a very good time it was there was a moocow coming down along the road and this moocow that was coming down along the road met a nicens little boy named baby tuckoo. [7]

Our knowledge of Stephen is now going to come to us mediated through his own developing consciousness. That consciousness is to be the theatre of whatever drama the book attempts to present, and at the same time a territory sufficiently broad for the exercise of the vigorous naturalism which Joyce has been learning from continental masters. Yet with a quite bare naturalism he is no longer to be content, and on the second page we come upon him putting unobtrusively into operation a different sort of machinery:

> The Vances lived in number seven. They had a different father and mother. They were Eileen's father and mother. When they were grown up he was going to marry Eileen. He hid under the table. His mother said:—O, Stephen will apologise.
>
> Dante said:
>
> —O, if not, the eagles will come and pull out his eyes.—
>
> > Pull out his eyes,
> > Apologise,
> > Apologise,
> > Pull out his eyes. [8]

The whole *Portrait* is an apologia: at the same time its cardinal assertion is that Stephen will *not* apologize; rather he awaits the eagles. Joyce's eyes, moreover, were in actual fact threatened from the first; presently in the *Portrait* Stephen as a schoolboy is going to be unjustly punished as a consequence of defective vision; the master who beats him makes an observation suggesting that his guilt is to be seen in his eye; the complex of ideas thus established remains with Stephen and is several times resumed in *Ulysses*—in a manner fully intelligible only to a reader equipped with the relevant memories of the *Portrait*. This technique of weaving elusive symbolic themes percurrently through the strongly realistic fabric of his writing is something that Joyce is to exploit more and more. His prose at length becomes a vast hall of echoes—and one fatally adapted (the toiling inquirer must feel) to the conflicting voices of scholiasts. Eventually Joyce appears to have enjoyed playing up to his commentators. 'Eins within a space,' we read in *Finnegans Wake,* 'and a wearywide space it wast, ere wohned a Mookse.' The relationship of the mookse to the moocow opens a wide field for conjecture.

The development of young men destined to be artists was already in Britain, as on the Continent, a prolific field of fiction, but this scarcely qualifies the large originality of the *Portrait,* which is as much a landmark in the English novel as is *Joseph Andrews* or *Middlemarch* or *The Way of All Flesh.* We have only to think of that novel's line of representative young men—Roderick Random, Tom Jones, David Copperfield, Arthur Pendennis, Richard Feverel—to realize that Stephen Dedalus is presented to us with a hitherto unexampled intimacy and immediacy. It is true that this is achieved at some cost to the vitality of the book as a whole. Here, as later in parts of *Ulysses,*

we are locked up firmly inside Stephen's head; and there are times
when we feel like shouting to be let out. What Stephen takes for
granted, we have to take for granted too; and as he is aware of other
people only as they affect his own interior chemistry, there is often
something rather shadowy about the remaining personages in the
book. But the picture is always clear and hard in its exhibition of
Stephen's successive predicaments. The imaginative and unathletic
small boy, hard-pressed by the narrow orthodoxies and hovering bru-
talities of a Jesuit boarding-school; his growing realization of his
family's drift into squalor, and the pride and arrogance which he
progressively summons to his aid; the overwhelming sense of sin into
which the severity of Catholic doctrine precipitates him upon the occasion of his untimely sexual initiation; the breaking of his nerve and
his phase of anxious and elaborate religious observance; his stumbling
but implacable advance, through reverie and through conversation
with whatever acquaintances will listen, upon an understanding of
the realm of art and his elected place in it; the crisis of his break with
Church and family, and the exalting moment of revelation and dedication on the strand: all these are vividly realized and rendered experiences.

In the *Portrait* Joyce abandons that aggressively frugal and monoto-
nous prose, pervasive in *Stephen Hero,* out of which he had evolved
the highly expressive 'scrupulous meanness' of *Dubliners.* Vocabulary,
syntax, rhythm are now boldly varied to accentuate the contours of
the underlying emotion, and Joyce is thus beginning to deploy his
resources as a master of imitative form. *Ulysses,* considered in point
of prose style, is to reveal itself quite frankly as a museum displaying,
as in a series of show-cases, all the old ways of using English and a
great many new ones as well. The *Portrait,* although in some degree
looking forward to this, renders an overriding impression of unity,
since each of the styles reflects one facet of Stephen, who is a highly
unified creation. 'He chronicled with patience what he saw,' we are
told, 'detaching himself from it and tasting its mortifying flavour in
secret.' This Stephen is best represented in some of the conversations—
which, as in *Dubliners,* are based upon an ear and intellect so alert
as to combine a maximum of significant statement with a minimum
of apparent selection. The early scene in which Stephen's father and
Mrs. Riordan quarrel over Irish politics during dinner on Christmas
day is Joyce's early masterpiece in this kind. When Stephen ceases
to be merely a recording intelligence, and responds actively to the
challenge of a world he finds so largely inimical, the style reaches out
at once for weapons and armour, its whole tone becoming an extension of Stephen's most caustic and arrogant condemnations; of Dublin
which has 'shrunk with time to a faint mortal odour,' of Ireland 'the
old sow that eats her farrow,' of her church which is 'the scullery-maid

of christendom.' Stephen himself is 'a priest of the eternal imagination,' and he speaks in cold exalted phrases consonant with the role.

But there is yet another Stephen in the book, the Stephen who
ceaselessly communes with himself on solitary walks about Dublin. It
is here—it is in the style Joyce largely employs in rendering Stephen
chez lui—that the success of the *Portrait* trembles in the balance. The
hazard is not the consequence of any simple miscalculation of effect;
it is a necessary risk involved in the complexity of what Joyce attempts. There are always two lights at play on Stephen. In the one
he is seen as veritably possessing the sanctity and strength he claims—
for he has been set aside, not of his own will, to serve the highest.
In the other he is only the eldest of Simon Dedalus's neglected children, and his aspirations have the pathos he is to discern in his sister
Dilly, when she shyly produces the tattered French grammar she has
bought from a stall. Moreover he is an adolescent as well as an artist;
and the emotions of adolescence are often both disturbingly self-
indulgent and much in excess of their specific precipitating occasions—expressing themselves in maudlin tags, conventional postures,
phrases and cadences caught up out of books, sometimes hovering
agonizingly between sublimity and absurdity, hysteria and inspiration.
It is because of all this that Stephen is represented as outrageously
sentimentalizing himself and regularly clothing his poignantly felt
nakedness in the faded splendours of a bygone poetic rhetoric:

> He heard the choir of voices in the kitchen echoed and multiplied
> through an endless reverberation of the choirs of endless generations
> of children and heard in all the echoes an echo also of the recurring
> note of weariness and pain. All seemed weary of life even before entering
> upon it. And he remembered that Newman had heard this note also in
> the broken lines of Virgil, *giving utterance, like the voice of Nature her-
> self, to that pain and weariness yet hope of better things which has been
> the experience of her children in every time.* [164]

In this kind of writing the key is regularly pitched not to the objective
scale of its occasion, but to the dimensions of that occasion as they
exist at the moment for the boy. Thus Stephen takes part in some
theatricals in the presence of the girl he admires, and the situation
excites and disturbs him. So we have:

> He hardly knew where he was walking. Pride and hope and desire
> like crushed herbs in his heart sent up vapours of maddening incense
> before the eyes of his mind. He strode down the hill amid the tumult
> of sudden risen vapours of wounded pride and fallen hope and baffled
> desire. They streamed upwards before his anguished eyes in dense and
> maddening fumes and passed away above him till at last the air was
> clear and cold again. [86]

Before places like this, or those far more highly wrought pages of the same sort which describe the boy's miserable frequenting of the brothels of the city, one of Joyce's best critics is surely wrong in speaking of 'purple passages that have faded considerably.' They remain highly expressive, like Juliet's hysteria or Hamlet's rant in Ophelia's grave.

At the book's crisis this boldly heightened writing is employed with great skill. Stephen's coming to his true vocation is by way of successive sensuous impressions each of which has a sort of trigger action upon forces which have been building themselves up in his mind. The piety which he has evinced since abandoning and repenting his carnal sins has suggested that he is apt for the priesthood, and the question of whether he has indeed a vocation is put to him temperately and wisely by a Jesuit director. His pride and arrogance are brought into play; he is tempted by the thought of secret knowledge and power. He is tempted, too, without clearly knowing it, as an artist: the 'vague acts of the priesthood' attract him 'by reason of their semblance of reality and of their distance from it.' On the threshold of the college the director gives Stephen his hand 'as if already to a companion in the spiritual life.' But Stephen feels the caress of a mild evening air, sees a group of young men walking with linked arms, hears a drift of music from a concertina. And these impressions are reinforced by memories of his schooldays:

> His lungs dilated and sank as if he were inhaling a warm moist unsustaining air and he smelt again the moist warm air which hung in the bath in Clongowes above the sluggish turfcoloured water.
> Some instinct, waking at these memories, stronger than education or piety, quickened within him at every near approach to that life, an instinct subtle and hostile, and armed him against acquiescence. [161]

Yet still his mind oscillates. He is entered at the university, and celebrates the occasion with comical portentousness in an elaborately harmonious reverie. But this in turn brings to his mind 'a proud cadence from Newman'—

> Whose feet are as the feet of harts and underneath the everlasting arms [165]

—and 'the pride of that dim image brought back to his mind the dignity of the office he had refused . . . The oils of ordination would never anoint his body. He had refused.' Why? The answer—the positive answer—comes as he walks on the beach. It is, in fact, the secular artist's reply to the 'proud cadence' of Newman:

> He drew forth a phrase from his treasure and spoke it softly to himself:
> —A day of dappled seaborne clouds. [166]

This is Stephen Dedalus's moment of apocalypse. He realizes that he has apprehended something beautiful. Soon he will be able to write in his diary the final truth about himself: 'I desire to press in my arms the loveliness which has not yet come into the world.' It is only a shallow irony that would remark that this loveliness is to be represented by Leopold and Molly Bloom in *Ulysses*. Nor need we contemn, in the name of sophisticated restraint, the pitch of the prose in which this moment, a moment at once of final release and final submission, is celebrated:

> Where was his boyhood now? Where was the soul that had hung back from her destiny, to brood alone upon the shame of her wounds and in her house of squalor and subterfuge to queen it in faded cerements and in wreaths that withered at the touch? Or where was he?
>
> He was alone. He was unheeded, happy and near to the wild heart of life. He was alone and young and wilful and wildhearted, alone amid a waste of wild air and brackish waters and the sea-harvest of shells and tangle and veiled grey sunlight and gayclad lightclad figures of children and girls and voices childish and girlish in the air. [171]

The whole hymn of praise and dedication and pride has still its aspect of precariousness and pathos; preserves, for all its gorgeousness, the poignancy of the boy's cry in *Stephen Hero*: 'Mother . . . I'm young, healthy, happy. What is the crying for?' Stephen, in a last analysis, is singing only as his brothers and sisters have been singing a few pages earlier, when that could be detected in their voices which Newman had heard in the broken lines of Virgil.

Stephen Hero

by Joseph Prescott

Stephen Hero is an absorbing document, straightforward, explicit, and marked by a fullness of statement which Joyce, for various reasons, denied to the *Portrait*.

Covering about two of Stephen's university years, what we have of *Stephen Hero* has a better claim to the title *A Portrait of the Artist as a Young Man* than does the so-miscalled work, which treats Stephen's experience from his earliest memories to young manhood. The 383 pages of manuscript,[1] as the editor points out, coincide with the last 93 pages of the *Portrait*. In both versions Stephen is the same poor, arrogant, and solitary young man. The hero who, invited to contribute to a college review, asks, "And tell me, will I be paid?" is recognizable as the young man who, when invited to sign a testimonial for universal peace, asks, "—Will you pay me anything if I sign?" The hero who expects "reward from the public for [his] verses because [he] believe[s his] verses are to be numbered among the spiritual assets of the State" is recognizable as the young man who goes forth "to forge in the smithy of [his] soul the uncreated conscience of [his] race." And the hero who "professed scorn for the rabblement and contempt for authority," had a "commandment of reticence," "was very lonely," and lived "such a strange life—without help or sympathy

[1] The 1955 edition of *Stephen Hero* incorporates the text of twenty-five additional manuscript pages, edited with a foreword by John J. Slocum and Herbert Cahoon. The text of five more pages of manuscript is made available by Slocum and Cahoon in Marvin Magalaner, ed., *A James Joyce Miscellany: Second Series* (Carbondale [Illinois], 1959), and in the 1963 edition of *Stephen Hero*. For first publication of the original version of the *Portrait*, a brief narrative essay antecedent to *Stephen Hero*, see R. M. Kain and R. E. Scholes, eds., "The First Version of Joyce's 'Portrait,'" *Yale Review*, XLIX (1960), 355–69. For an annotated edition of the first version, see Robert Scholes and Richard M. Kain, *The Workshop of Daedalus: James Joyce and the Raw Materials for A Portrait of the Artist as a Young Man* (Evanston, Illinois, 1965), pp. 56–74.

from anyone" that "sometimes [he was] afraid of [himself]" is recognizable as the young man who felt keenly "that he was different from others," who "was happy only when he was . . . alone or in the company of phantasmal comrades," who "was destined to learn his own wisdom apart from others or to learn the wisdom of others himself wandering among the snares of the world."

It is notable that the youthful preferences which Joyce records in *Stephen Hero* are perhaps more significant than those he mentions in the *Portrait*. In *Stephen Hero,* as is not the case in the *Portrait,* we have a revealing account of Stephen's devotion to two artists. Of the first, Joyce begins: "It must be said simply and at once that at this time Stephen suffered the most enduring influence of his life." And Ibsen plays a central role in Stephen's experience, for it is in defense of him, in connection with a paper on "Art and Life" read before the University College Literary and Historical Society, that Stephen breaks a lance with the authority for which, as an artist, he professes contempt. Furthermore, in March, 1901, the nineteen-year-old Joyce wrote to Ibsen personally, praising "your highest excellence— your lofty impersonal power . . . and how in your absolute indifference to public canons of art, friends and shibboleths you walked in the light of your inward *heroism*." In October of the same year Joyce wrote, in the essay *The Day of the Rabblement*: "No man, said the Nolan, can be a lover of the true or the good unless he abhors the multitude; and the artist, though he may employ the crowd, is very careful to isolate himself"; he remarked that "every movement [of protest against the sterility and falsehood of the modern stage] that has set out *heroically* has achieved a little"; and he spoke reverently of "the old master who is dying in Christiania." I have italicized the words *heroism* and *heroically* for, written when *Stephen Hero* was presumably already in process of gestation, they indicate the turn of the author's thought at the time: Ibsen is a hero, and opposition to sterility and falsehood is the act of heroes to the prototype of Stephen the hero.

Of the second artist whose work Stephen admired, Joyce begins:

[Stephen] had found on one of the carts of books near the river an unpublished book containing two stories by W. B. Yeats. One of these stories was called *The Tables of the Law* . . . and one evening while talking with a Capuchin, he had over and over to restrain an impulse which urged him to take the priest by the arm, lead him up and down the chapel-yard and deliver himself boldly of the whole story of *The Tables of the Law,* every word of which he remembered. . . . He satisfied himself by leading Lynch round the enclosure of Stephen's Green and making that young man very awkward by reciting Mr Yeats's story with careful animation. . . . He repeated often the story of *The Tables of the Law* and the story of the *Adoration of the Magi*. [*SH,* 176–178]

Later, quotations from both stories are put into Stephen's mouth. And a further measure of Joyce's attachment to these stories is anonymously indicated in Yeats's prefatory note to the first public edition: "These two stories were privately printed some years ago. I do not think I should have reprinted them had I not met a young man in Ireland the other day, who liked them very much and nothing else that I have written." The young man, according to Yeats's biographer, Joseph Hone, was Joyce.

The leading characters of both stories stand outside established orders. Both artists whom Stephen and his creator find congenial are proud preachers of independence of social taboos. Joyce-Dedalus bears out a statement which Dedalus is later to make in *Ulysses*: "We walk through ourselves, meeting robbers, ghosts, giants, old men, young men, wives, widows, brothers-in-love. But always meeting ourselves."

Stephen's character as I have said, is essentially the same in both versions. What changes is the relationship between that character and the author. This is perhaps the most important qualitative difference between the two versions.

A fair illustration of the attitude of the author to his subject in *Stephen Hero* is the introductory sentence, already quoted, about Ibsen (whom, it will be remembered, Joyce admired for his impersonality): "It must be said simply and at once that at this time Stephen suffered the most enduring influence of his life." Here is the author not merely reporting a fact regarding his character but also, by his strident emphasis, announcing his own position. Other brief editorial asides ("it is as well to admit that"—"undoubtedly") leave the reader no choice but to listen to the author's explicit point of view. The editorial phrase extends to sententious and abstract generalization:

> This quality of the mind which so reveals itself is called (when incorrigible) a decadence but if we are to take a general view of . . . the world we cannot but see a process to life through corruption. . . . When a demand for intelligent sympathy goes unanswered . . . he is a too stern disciplinarian who blames himself for having offered a dullard an opportunity to participate in the warmer movement of a more highly organized life. . . . No young man can contemplate the fact of death with extreme satisfaction and no young man, specialised by fate or her stepsister chance for an organ of sensitiveness and intellectiveness, can contemplate the network of falsities and trivialities which make up the funeral of a dead burgher without extreme disgust.

The tendency to editorialize reaches a peak, as one might expect, at a peak of emotion, and phrase and sentence are, in one instance, elaborated into a long and tense essay. Joyce has been reporting Stephen's thoughts on Catholicism.

That kind of Christianity which is called Catholicism seemed to him to stand in his way and forthwith he removed it. He had been brought up in the belief of the Roman supremacy and to cease to be a Catholic for him meant to cease to be a Christian.

Then, almost imperceptibly, Joyce crosses the vague line between autobiographical creation and creator:

The idea that the power of an empire is weakest at its borders requires some modification for everyone knows that the Pope cannot govern Italy as he governs Ireland nor is the Tsar as terrible an engine to the tradesmen of S. Petersburg as he is to the little Russian of the Steppes. In fact in many cases the government of an empire is strongest at its borders and it is invariably strongest there in the case when its power at the centre is on the wane. The waves of the rise and fall of empires do not travel with the rapidity of waves of light and it will be perhaps a considerable time before Ireland will be able to understand that the Papacy is no longer going through a period of anabolism. The bands of pilgrims who are shepherded safely across the continent by their Irish pastors must shame the jaded reactionaries of the eternal city by their stupefied intensity of worship in much the same way as the staring pro-vincial newly arrived from Spain or Africa may have piqued the loyalty of some smiling Roman for whom . . . the future of his race was be-coming uncertain as its past had already become obvious. Though it is evident on the one hand that this persistence of Catholic power in Ire-land must intensify very greatly the loneliness of the Irish Catholic who voluntarily outlaws himself yet on the other hand the force which he must generate to propel himself out of so strong and intricate a tyranny may often be sufficient to place him beyond the region of re-attraction.

Again almost imperceptibly, Joyce crosses back from himself to his autobiographical creation:

It was, in fact, the very fervour of Stephen's former religious life which sharpened for him now the pains of his solitary position and at the same time hardened into a less pliable, a less appeasable enmity molten rages and glowing transports on which the emotions of helplessness and loneli-ness and despair had first acted as chilling influences.

It needed only a change of tense to transform the authorial essay into an organic part of Stephen's experience. But the young Joyce had not yet sufficiently detached himself from his own thoughts and feelings to give them to his not much younger creation. He failed, in other words, to achieve the "esthetic stasis" which Stephen regards as es-sential to the success of a work of art. "The artist, like the God of the creation," Stephen says in the *Portrait*, "remains within or behind or beyond or above his handiwork, invisible, refined out of existence, indifferent, paring his fingernails.—" In *Stephen Hero* a tone of ado-lescently turbulent rancor, everywhere audible, inspires the reader with loathing for "Irish paralysis"—a "kinetic" effect, which, according to Stephen's esthetic, makes for improper art. We may, in fact, say of the author of this early version what he says in it of his titular character: "It was hard for him to compel his head to preserve the strict temperature of classicism."

In the *Portrait*, on the other hand, from start to finish there is not a single comment or generalization; every thought, every feeling is particularly Stephen's. Now and then, to be sure, the author *reports* as author, but he never *comments*. "It was the very spirit of Ibsen himself," Joyce wrote in *Stephen Hero*, "that was discerned moving behind the impersonal manner of the artist"; so, again to be sure, it is the very spirit of Joyce himself that is discerned moving behind the impersonal manner of the artist of the *Portrait*. But such discernibleness is not inconsistent with the invisibility of the God of the creation behind his handiwork.

At this point the evolution of Joyce's novel becomes interesting beyond itself, for the history of this novel repeats the history of the genre. The change from *Stephen Hero* to the *Portrait* mirrors the progression from the novel of the overt and partisan manager to that of the invisible and impersonal director.

The *Portrait* in Perspective

by Hugh Kenner

The "instant of emotion" [214] of which this 300-page lyric is the "simplest verbal vesture" is the exalted instant, emerging at the end of the book, of freedom, of vocation, of Stephen's destiny, winging his way above the waters at the side of the hawklike man: the instant of promise on which the crushing ironies of *Ulysses* are to fall. The epic of the sea of matter is preceded by the lyric image of a growing dream: a dream that like Richard Rowan's in *Exiles* disregards the fall of man; a dream nourished by a sensitive youth of flying above the sea into an uncreated heaven:

> The spell of arms and voices: the white arms of roads, their promise of close embraces and the black arms of tall ships that stand against the moon, their tale of distant nations. They are held out to say: We are alone—come. And the voices say with them: We are your kinsmen. And the air is thick with their company as they call to me, their kinsman, making ready to go, shaking the wings of their exultant and terrible youth. [252]

The emotional quality of this is continuous with that of the *Count of Monte Cristo,* that fantasy of the exile returned for vengeance (the plot of the *Odyssey*) which kindled so many of Stephen's boyhood dreams:

> The figure of that dark avenger stood forth in his mind for whatever he had heard or divined in childhood of the strange and terrible. At night he built up on the parlour table an image of the wonderful island cave out of transfers and paper flowers and strips of the silver and golden paper in which chocolate is wrapped. When he had broken up this scenery, weary of its tinsel, there would come to his mind the bright picture of Marseilles, of sunny trellises and of Mercedes. [62]

The prose surrounding Stephen's flight is empurpled with transfers and paper flowers too. It is not immature prose, as we might suppose by comparison with *Ulysses*. The prose of "The Dead" is mature prose, and "The Dead" was written in 1908. Rather, it is a meticulous pastiche of immaturity. Joyce has his eye constantly on the epic sequel.

> He wanted to meet in the real world the unsubstantial image which his soul so constantly beheld. He did not know where to seek it or how, but a premonition which led him on told him that this image would, without any overt act of his, encounter him. They would meet quietly as if they had known each other and had made their tryst, perhaps at one of the gates or in some more secret place. They would be alone, surrounded by darkness and silence: and in that moment of supreme tenderness he would be transfigured. [65]

As the vaginal imagery of gates, secret places, and darkness implies, this is the dream that reaches temporary fulfilment in the plunge into profane love [100]. But the ultimate "secret place" is to be Mabbot Street, outside Bella Cohen's brothel; the unsubstantial image of his quest, that of Leopold Bloom, advertisement canvasser—Monte Cristo, returned avenger, Ulysses; and the transfiguration, into the phantasmal dead son of a sentimental Jew:

> *Against the dark wall a figure appears slowly, a fairy boy of eleven, a changeling, kidnapped, dressed in an Eton suit with glass shoes and a little bronze helmet, holding a book in his hand. He reads from right to left inaudibly, smiling, kissing the page.* [U, 593/609]

That Dedalus the artificer did violence to nature is the point of the epigraph from Ovid, *Et ignotas animum dimittit in artes;* the Icarian fall is inevitable.

> In tedious exile now too long detain'd
> Dedalus languish'd for his native land.
> The sea foreclos'd his flight; yet thus he said,
> Though earth and water in subjection laid,
> O cruel Minos, thy dominion be,
> We'll go through air; for sure the air is free.
> *Then to new arts his cunning thought applies,*
> *And to improve the work of nature tries.*

Stephen does not, as the careless reader may suppose, become an artist by rejecting church and country. Stephen does not become an artist at all. Country, church, and mission are an inextricable unity, and in rejecting the two that seem to hamper him, he rejects also the one on which he has set his heart. Improving the work of nature is his obvious ambition ("But you could not have a green rose. But perhaps somewhere in the world you could"), and it logically follows from the aesthetic he expounds to Lynch. It is a neo-platonic aesthetic; the crucial principle of epiphanization has been withdrawn. He imagines that "the loveliness that has not yet come into the world" [251] is to be found in his own soul. The earth is gross, and what it brings forth is cowdung; sound and shape and colour are "the prison gates of our

soul"; and beauty is something mysteriously gestated within. The genuine artist reads signatures, the fake artist forges them, a process adumbrated in the obsession of Shem the Penman (from *Jim the Penman*,
a forgotten drama about a forger) with "Macfearsome's Ossean," the
most famous of literary forgeries, studying "how cutely to copy all
their various styles of signature so as one day to utter an epical forged
cheque on the public for his own private profit." [*F*, 181]

One can sense all this in the first four chapters of the *Portrait*, and
Ulysses is unequivocal:

> Fabulous artificer, the hawklike man. You flew. Whereto? Newhaven-
> Dieppe, steerage passenger. Paris and back. [*U*, 208/210]

The Stephen of the end of the fourth chapter, however, is still unstable;
he had to be brought into a final balance, and shown at some length as
a being whose development was virtually ended. Unfortunately, the
last chapter makes the book a peculiarly difficult one for the reader to
focus, because Joyce had to close it on a suspended chord. As a lyric,
it is finished in its own terms; but the themes of the last forty pages,
though they give the illusion of focussing, don't really focus until we
have read well into *Ulysses*. The final chapter, which in respect to the
juggernaut of *Ulysses* must be a vulnerable flank, in respect to what
has gone before must be a conclusion. This problem Joyce didn't wholly
solve; there remains a moral ambiguity (how seriously are we to take
Stephen?) which makes the last forty pages painful reading.

Not that Stephen would stand indefinitely if *Ulysses* didn't topple
him over; his equilibrium in Chapter V, though good enough to give
him a sense of unusual integrity in University College, is precarious
unless he can manage, in the manner of so many permanent under-
graduates, to prolong the college context for the rest of his life. Each
of the preceding chapters, in fact, works toward an equilibrium which
is dashed when in the next chapter Stephen's world becomes larger
and the frame of reference more complex. The terms of equilibrium
are always stated with disquieting accuracy; at the end of Chapter I
we find:

> He was alone. He was happy and free: but he would not be anyway
> proud with Father Dolan. He would be very quiet and obedient: and
> he wished that he could do something kind for him to show him that
> he was not proud. [59]

And at the end of Chapter III:

> He sat by the fire in the kitchen, not daring to speak for happiness.
> Till that moment he had not known how beautiful and peaceful life
> could be. The green square of paper pinned round the lamp cast down
> a tender shade. On the dresser was a plate of sausages and white pudding
> and on the shelf there were eggs. They would be for the breakfast in the
> morning after the communion in the college chapel. White pudding and

eggs and sausages and cups of tea. How simple and beautiful was life after all! And life lay all before him. [146]

Not "irony" but simply the truth: the good life conceived in terms of white pudding and sausages is unstable enough to need no under-lining.

The even-numbered chapters make a sequence of a different sort. The ending of IV, Stephen's panting submission to an artistic voca-tion:

> Evening had fallen when he woke and the sand and arid grasses of his bed glowed no longer. He rose slowly and, recalling the rapture of his sleep, sighed at its joy. . . . [173]

—hasn't quite the finality often read into it when the explicit parallel with the ending of II is perceived:

> . . . He closed his eyes, surrendering himself to her, body and mind, conscious of nothing in the world but the dark pressure of her softly parting lips. They pressed upon his brain as upon his lips as though they were the vehicle of a vague speech; and between them he felt an unknown and timid pressure, darker than the swoon of sin, softer than sound or odour. [101]

When we link these passages with the fact that the one piece of literary composition Stephen actually achieves in the book comes out of a wet dream ("Towards dawn he awoke. O what sweet music! His soul was all dewy wet," [217]) we are in a position to see that the concluding "Welcome, O life!" has an air of finality and balance only because the diary-form of the last seven pages disarms us with an illusion of aucto-rial impartiality.

Ego *vs.* authority is the theme of the three odd-numbered chapters, Dublin *vs.* the dream that of the two even-numbered ones. The generic Joyce plot, the encounter with the alter ego, is consummated when Stephen at the end of the book identifies himself with the sanctified Stephen who was stoned by the Jews after reporting a vision (Acts VII, 56) and claims sonship with the classical Daedalus who evaded the ruler of land and sea by turning his soul to obscure arts. The episodes are built about adumbrations of this encounter: with Father Conmee, with Monte Cristo, with the whores, with the broad-shouldered moustached student who cut the word "Foetus" in a desk, with the weary mild confessor, with the bird-girl. Through this repeated plot interwine con-trolling emotions and controlling images that mount in complexity as the book proceeds.

In Chapter I the controlling emotion is fear, and the dominant image Father Dolan and his pandybat; this, associated with the hang-man-god and the priestly denial of the senses, was to become one of

Joyce's standard images for Irish clericalism—hence the jack-in-the-box appearance of Father Dolan in Circe's nightmare imbroglio, his pandybat cracking twice like thunder. [*U*, 547/561] Stephen's comment, in the mode of Blake's repudiation of the God who slaughtered Jesus, emphasizes the inclusiveness of the image: "I never could read His handwriting except His criminal thumbprint on the haddock."

Chapter II opens with a triple image of Dublin's prepossessions: music, sport, religion. The first is exhibited via Uncle Charles singing sentimental ballads in the outhouse; the second via Stephen's ritual run around the park under the eye of a superannuated trainer, which his uncle enjoins on him as the whole duty of a Dubliner; the third via the clumsy piety of Uncle Charles, kneeling on a red handkerchief and reading above his breath "from a thumbblackened prayerbook wherein catchwords were printed at the foot of every page." [62] This trinity of themes is unwound and entwined throughout the chapter, like a net woven round Stephen; it underlies the central incident, the Whitsuntide play in the Belvedere chapel (religion), which opens with a display by the dumb-bell team (sport) preluded by sentimental waltzes from the soldier's band (music).

While he is waiting to play his part, Stephen is taunted by fellow-students, who rally him on a fancied love-affair and smiting his calf with a cane bid him recite the *Confiteor*. His mind goes back to an analogous incident, when a similar punishment had been visited on his refusal to "admit that Byron was no good." The further analogy with Father Dolan is obvious; love, art, and personal independence are thus united in an ideogram of the prepossessions Stephen is determined to cultivate in the teeth of persecution.

The dream-world Stephen nourishes within himself is played against manifestations of music, sport, and religion throughout the chapter. The constant ironic clash of Dublin *vs.* the Dream animates Chapter II, as the clash of the ego *vs.* authority did Chapter I. All these themes come to focus during Stephen's visit with his father to Cork. The dream of rebellion he has silently cultivated is externalized by the discovery of the word *Foetus* carved in a desk by a forgotten medical student:

> It shocked him to find in the outer world a trace of what he had deemed till then a brutish and individual malady of his own mind. His monstrous reveries came thronging into his memory. They too had sprung up before him, suddenly and furiously, out of mere words. . . . [90]

The possibility of shame gaining the upper hand is dashed, however, by the sudden banal intrusion of his father's conversation ("When you kick out for yourself, Stephen, as I daresay you will one of these days, remember, whatever you do, to mix with gentlemen . . ."). Against the standards of Dublin his monstrous reveries acquire a Satanic glamour, and the trauma is slowly diverted into a resolution to rebel. After his father has expressed a resolve to "leave him to his Maker" (religion), and offered to "sing a tenor song against him" (music) or "vault a five-barred gate against him" (sport), Stephen muses, watching his father and two cronies drinking to the memory of their past:

> An abyss of fortune or of temperament sundered him from them. His mind seemed older than theirs: it shone coldly on their strifes and happiness and regrets like a moon upon a younger earth. No life or youth stirred in him as it had stirred in them. He had known neither the pleasure of companionship with others nor the vigour of rude male health nor filial piety. Nothing stirred within his soul but a cold and cruel and loveless lust. [95–96]

After one final effort to compromise with Dublin on Dublin's terms has collapsed into futility ("The pot of pink enamel paint gave out and the wainscot of his bedroom remained with its unfinished and ill-plastered coat" [98]), he fiercely cultivates his rebellious thoughts, and moving by day and night "among distorted images of the outer world," [99] plunges at last into the arms of whores. "The holy encounter he had then imagined at which weakness and timidity and inexperience were to fall from him" [99] finally arrives in inversion of Father Dolan's and Uncle Charles' religion: his descent into night-town is accompanied by lurid evocations of a Black Mass (Cf. *Ulysses*, 583/599):

> The yellow gasflames arose before his troubled vision against the vapoury sky, burning as if before an altar. Before the doors and in the lighted halls groups were gathered arrayed as for some rite. He was in another world: he had awakened from a slumber of centuries. [100]

Each chapter in the *Portrait* gathers up the thematic material of the preceding ones and entwines them with a dominant theme of its own. In Chapter III the fear-pandybat motif is present in Father Arnall's crudely materialistic hell, of which even the thickness of the walls is specified; and the Dublin-*vs.*-dream motif has ironic inflections in Stephen's terror-stricken broodings, when the dream has been twisted into a dream of holiness, and even Dublin appears transfigured:

> How beautiful must be a soul in the state of grace when God looked upon it with love!
> Frowsy girls sat along the curbstones before their baskets. Their dank hair trailed over their brows. They were not beautiful to see as they crouched in the mire. But their souls were seen by God; and if their souls were in a state of grace they were radiant to see; and God loved them, seeing them. [140]

A *rapprochement* in these terms between the outer world and Stephen's desires is too inadequate to need commentary; and it makes vivid as nothing else could the hopeless inversion of his attempted self-sufficiency. It underlines, in yet another way, his persistent sin: and the

dominant theme of Chapter III is Sin. A fugue-like opening plays upon
the Seven Deadly Sins in turn; gluttony is in the first paragraph ("Stuff
it into you, his belly counselled him"), followed by lust, then sloth
("A cold lucid indifference reigned in his soul"), pride ("His pride in
his own sin, his loveless awe of God, told him that his offence was too
grievous to be atoned for"), anger ("The blundering answer stirred
the embers of his contempt for his fellows"); finally, a recapitulation
fixes each term of the mortal catalogue in a phrase, enumerating how
"from the evil seed of lust all the other deadly sins had sprung forth."
[106]
  Priest and punisher inhabit Stephen himself as well as Dublin: when
he is deepest in sin he is most thoroughly a theologian. A paragraph of
gloomy introspection is juxtaposed with a list of theological questions
that puzzle Stephen's mind as he awaits the preacher:

> . . . Is baptism with mineral water valid? How comes it that while the
> first beatitude promises the kingdom of heaven to the poor of heart,
> the second beatitude promises also to the meek that they shall possess the
> land? . . . If the wine change into vinegar and the host crumble into
> corruption after they have been consecrated, is Jesus Christ still present
> under their species as God and as man?
> —Here he is! Here he is!
> A boy from his post at the window had seen the rector come from the
> house. All the catechisms were opened and all heads bent upon them
> silently. [106–107]

Wine changed into vinegar and the host crumbled into corruption fits
exactly the Irish clergy of "a church which was the scullery-maid of
Christendom." The excited "Here he is! Here he is!" following hard
on the mention of Jesus Christ and signalling nothing more portentous
than the rector makes the point as dramatically as anything in the book,
and the clinching sentence, with the students suddenly bending over
their catechisms, places the rector as the vehicle of pandybat morality.
  The last of the theological questions is the telling question. Stephen
never expresses doubt of the existence of God nor of the essential
validity of the priestly office—his *Non serviam* is not a *non credo,* and
he talks of a "malevolent reality" behind these appearances [243]—but
the wine and bread that were offered for his veneration were changed
into vinegar and crumbled into corruption. And it was the knowledge of that underlying validity clashing with his refusal to do hom-
age to vinegar and rot that evoked his ambivalent poise of egocentric
despair. The hell of Father Arnall's sermon, so emotionally overwhelming, so picayune beside the horrors that Stephen's imagination can
generate, had no more ontological content for Stephen that had "an
eternity of bliss in the company of the dean of studies." [240]
  The conflict of this central chapter is again between the phantasmal
and the real. What is real—psychologically real, because realized—is

Stephen's anguish and remorse, and its context in the life of the flesh. What is phantasmal is the "heaven" of the Church and the "good life" of the priest. It is only fear that makes him clutch after the latter at all; his reaching out after orthodox salvation is, as we have come to expect, presented in terms that judge it:

> The wind blew over him and passed on to the myriads and myriads of other souls, on whom God's favour shone now more and now less, stars now brighter and now dimmer, sustained and failing. And the glimmering souls passed away, sustained and failing, merged in a moving breath. One soul was lost; a tiny soul; his. It flickered once and went out, forgotten, lost. The end: black cold void waste.
>
> Consciousness of place came ebbing back to him slowly over a vast tract of time unlit, unfelt, unlived. The squalid scene composed itself around him; the common accents, the burning gasjets in the shops, odours of fish and spirits and wet sawdust, moving men and women. An old woman was about to cross the street, an oilcan in her hand. He bent down and asked her was there a chapel near. [140–141]

That wan waste world of flickering stars is the best Stephen has been able to do towards an imaginative grasp of the communion of Saints sustained by God; "unlit, unfelt, unlived" explains succinctly why it had so little hold on him, once fear had relaxed. Equally pertinent is the vision of human temporal occupations the sermon evokes:

> What did it profit a man to gain the whole world if he lost his soul? At last he had understood: and human life lay around him, a plain of peace whereon antlike men laboured in brotherhood, their dead sleeping under quiet mounds. [126]

To maintain the life of grace in the midst of nature, sustained by so cramped a vision of the life of nature, would mean maintaining an intolerable tension. Stephen's unrelenting philosophic bias, his determination to understand what he is about, precludes his adopting the double standard of the Dubliners; to live both the life of nature and the life of grace he must enjoy an imaginative grasp of their relationship which stunts neither. "No one doth well against his will," writes Saint Augustine, "even though what he doth, be well;" and Stephen's will is firmly harnessed to his understanding. And there is no one in Dublin to help him achieve understanding. Father Arnall's sermon precludes rather than secures a desirable outcome, for it follows the modes of pandybat morality and Dublin materiality. Its only possible effect on Stephen is to lash his dormant conscience into a frenzy. The description of Hell as "a strait and dark and foul smelling prison, an abode of demons and lost souls, filled with fire and smoke," with walls four thousand miles thick, its damned packed in so tightly that "they are not even able to remove from the eye the worm that gnaws it," is childishly grotesque beneath its sweeping eloquence; and the hair-

splitting catalogues of pains—pain of loss, pain of conscience (divided
into three heads), pain of extension, pain of intensity, pain of eternity
—is cast in a brainlessly analytic mode that effectively prevents any
corresponding Heaven from possessing any reality at all.

Stephen's unstable pact with the Church, and its dissolution, follows
the pattern of composition and dissipation established by his other
dreams: the dream for example of the tryst with "Mercedes," which
found ironic reality among harlots. It parallels exactly his earlier
attempt to "build a breakwater of order and elegance against the
sordid tide of life without him" [98] whose failure, with the exhaus-
tion of his money, was epiphanized in the running-dry of a pot of pink
enamel paint. His regimen at that time:

> He bought presents for everyone, overhauled his rooms, wrote out reso-
> lutions, marshalled his books up and down their shelves, pored over all
> kinds of price lists . . .

is mirrored by his searching after spiritual improvement:

> His daily life was laid out in devotional areas. By means of ejaculations
> and prayers he stored up ungrudgingly for the souls in purgatory centu-
> ries of days and quarantines and years. . . . He offered up each of his
> three daily chaplets that his soul might grow strong in each of the three
> theological virtues. . . . On each of the seven days of the week he further
> prayed that one of the seven gifts of the Holy Ghost might descend upon
> his soul. [147–148]

The "loan bank" he had opened for the family, out of which he had
pressed loans on willing borrowers "that he might have the pleasure
of making out receipts and reckoning the interests on sums lent" finds
its counterpart in the benefits he stored up for souls in purgatory that
he might enjoy the spiritual triumph of "achieving with ease so many
fabulous ages of canonical penances." Both projects are parodies on the
doctrine of economy of grace; both are attempts, corrupted by motivat-
ing self-interest, to make peace with Dublin on Dublin's own terms;
and both are short-lived.

As this precise analogical structure suggests, the action of each of
the five chapters is really the same action. Each chapter closes with a
synthesis of triumph which the next destroys. The triumph of the
appeal to Father Conmee from lower authority, of the appeal to the
harlots from Dublin, of the appeal to the Church from sin, of the
appeal to art from the priesthood (the bird-girl instead of the Virgin)
is always the same triumph raised to a more comprehensive level. It is
an attempt to find new parents; new fathers in the odd chapters, new
objects of love in the even. The last version of Father Conmee is the
"priest of the eternal imagination"; the last version of Mercedes is
the "lure of the fallen seraphim." But the last version of the mother

who said, "O, Stephen will apologise" is the mother who prays on the last page "that I may learn in my own life and away from home and friends what the heart is and what it feels." The mother remains.

As in *Dubliners* and *Exiles*, the female role in the *Portrait* is less to arouse than to elucidate masculine desires. Hence the complex function in the book of physical love: the physical is the analogue of the spiritual, as St. Augustine insisted in his *Confessions* (which, with Ibsen's *Brand*, is the chief archetype of Joyce's book). The poles between which this affection moves are those of St. Augustine and St. John: the Whore of Babylon and the Bride of Christ. The relation between the two is far from simple, and Stephen moves in a constant tension between them.

His desire, figured in the visions of Monte Cristo's Mercedes, "to meet in the real world the unsubstantial image which his soul so constantly beheld" draws him toward the prostitute ("In her arms he felt that he had suddenly become strong and fearless and sure of himself" [101]) and simultaneously toward the vaguely spiritual satisfaction represented with equal vagueness by the wraithlike E— C—, to whom he twice writes verses. The Emma Clery of *Stephen Hero,* with her loud forced manners and her body compact of pleasure [*SH*, 66], was refined into a wraith with a pair of initials to parallel an intangible Church. She is continually assimilated to the image of the Blessed Virgin and of the heavenly Bride. The torture she costs him is the torture his apostasy costs him. His flirtation with her is his flirtation with Christ. His profane villanelle draws its imagery from religion—the incense, the eucharistic hymn, the chalice—and her heart, following Dante's image, is a rose, and in her praise "the earth was like a swinging swaying censer, a ball of incense." [218]

The woman is the Church. His vision of greeting Mercedes with "a sadly proud gesture of refusal":

—Madam, I never eat muscatel grapes. [63]

is fulfilled when he refuses his Easter communion. Emma's eyes, in their one explicit encounter, speak to him from beneath a cowl. [69] "The glories of Mary held his soul captive," [104] and a temporary reconciliation of his lust and his spiritual thirst is achieved as he reads the Lesson out of the Song of Solomon. In the midst of his repentance she functions as imagined mediator: "The image of Emma appeared before him," and, repenting, "he imagined that he stood near Emma in a wide land, and, humbly and in tears, bent and kissed the elbow of her sleeve." [116] Like Dante's Beatrice, she manifests in his earthly experience the Church Triumphant of his spiritual dream. And when he rejects her because she seems to be flirting with Father Moran, his anger is couched in the anti-clerical terms of his apostasy: "He had done well to leave her to flirt with her priest, to toy with a church which was the scullerymaid of christendom." [220]

That Kathleen ni Houlihan can flirt with priests is the unforgivable sin underlying Stephen's rejection of Ireland. But he makes a clear distinction between the stupid clericalism which makes intellectual and communal life impossible, and his long-nourished vision of an artist's Church Triumphant upon earth. He rejects the actual for daring to fall short of his vision.

The climax of the book is of course Stephen's ecstatic discovery of his vocation at the end of Chapter IV. The prose rises in nervous excitement to beat again and again the tambours of a fin-de-siècle ecstasy:

> His heart trembled; his breath came faster and a wild spirit passed over his limbs as though he were soaring sunward. His heart trembled in an ecstasy of fear and his soul was in flight. His soul was soaring in an air beyond the world and the body he knew was purified in a breath and delivered of incertitude and made radiant and commingled with the element of the spirit. An ecstasy of flight made radiant his eyes and wild his breath and tremulous and wild and radiant his windswept limbs.
>
> —One! Two! . . . Look out!—
> —O, Cripes, I'm drownded!—[169]

The interjecting voices of course are those of bathers, but their ironic appropriateness to Stephen's Icarian "soaring sunward" is not meant to escape us: divers have their own "ecstasy of flight," and Icarus was "drownded." The imagery of Stephen's ecstasy is fetched from many sources; we recognize Shelley's skylark, Icarus, the glorified body of the Resurrection (cf. "His soul had arisen from the grave of boyhood, spurning her graveclothes" [170]) and a tremulousness from which it is difficult to dissociate adolescent sexual dreams (which the Freudians tell us are frequently dreams of flying). The entire eight-page passage is cunningly organized with great variety of rhetoric and incident; but we cannot help noticing the limits set on vocabulary and figures of thought. The empurpled triteness of such a cadence as "radiant his eyes and wild his breath and tremulous and wild and radiant his windswept face" is enforced by recurrence: "But her long fair hair was girlish: and girlish, and touched with the wonder of mortal beauty, her face." [171] "Ecstasy" is the keyword, indeed. This riot of feelings corresponds to no vocation definable in mature terms; the paragraphs come to rest on images of irresponsible motion:

> He turned away from her suddenly and set off across the strand. His cheeks were aflame; his body was aglow; his limbs were trembling. On and on and on and on he strode, far out over the sands, singing wildly to the sea, crying to greet the advent of the life that had cried to him. [172]

What "life" connotes it skills not to ask; the word recurs and recurs. So does the motion onward and onward and onward:

> A wild angel had appeared to him, the angel of mortal youth and beauty, an envoy from the fair courts of life, to throw open before him in an instant of ecstasy the gates of all the ways of error and glory. On and on and on and on! [172]

It may be well to recall Joyce's account of the romantic temper:

> . . . an insecure, unsatisfied, impatient temper which sees no fit abode here for its ideals and chooses therefore to behold them under insensible figures. As a result of this choice it comes to disregard certain limitations. Its figures are blown to wild adventures, lacking the gravity of solid bodies. . . . [SH, 78]

Joyce also called *Prometheus Unbound* "the Schwärmerei of a young jew."

And it is quite plain from the final chapter of the *Portrait* that we are not to accept the mode of Stephen's "freedom" as the "message" of the book. The "priest of the eternal imagination" turns out to be indigestibly Byronic. Nothing is more obvious than his total lack of humour. The dark intensity of the first four chapters is moving enough, but our impulse on being confronted with the final edition of Stephen Dedalus is to laugh; and laugh at this moment we dare not; he is after all a victim being prepared for a sacrifice. His shape, as Joyce said, can no longer change. The art he has elected is not "the slow elaborative patience of the art of satisfaction." "On and on and on and on" will be its inescapable mode. He does not *see* the girl who symbolizes the full revelation; "she seemed like one whom magic had changed into the likeness of a strange and beautiful seabird," [171] and he confusedly apprehends a sequence of downy and feathery incantations. What, in the last chapter, he does see he sees only to reject, in favour of an incantatory "loveliness which has not yet come into the world." [251]

The only creative attitude to language exemplified in the book is that of Stephen's father:

> —Is it Christy? he said. There's more cunning in one of those warts on his bald head than in a pack of jack foxes.

His vitality is established before the book is thirty pages under way. Stephen, however, isn't enchanted at any time by the proximity of such talk. He isn't, as a matter of fact, even interested in it. Without a backward glance, he exchanges this father for a myth.

The Structure of the *Portrait*

by Richard Ellmann

To write *A Portrait of the Artist as a Young Man* Joyce plunged back into his own past, mainly to justify, but also to expose it. The book's pattern, as he explained to Stanislaus, is that we are what we were; our maturity is an extension of our childhood, and the courageous boy is father of the arrogant young man. But in searching for a way to convert the episodic *Stephen Hero* into *A Portrait of the Artist,* Joyce hit upon a principle of structure which reflected his habits of mind as extremely as he could wish. The work of art, like a mother's love, must be achieved over the greatest obstacles, and Joyce, who had been dissatisfied with his earlier work as too easily done, now found the obstacles in the form of a most complicated pattern.

This is hinted at in his image of the creative process. As far back as his paper on Mangan, Joyce said that the poet takes into the vital center of his life 'the life that surrounds it, flinging it abroad again amid planetary music.' He repeated this image in *Stephen Hero,* then in *A Portrait of the Artist* developed it more fully. Stephen refers to the making of literature as 'the phenomenon of artistic conception, artistic gestation and artistic reproduction,' and then describes the progression from lyrical to epical and to dramatic art:

> The simplest epical form is seen emerging out of lyrical literature when the artist prolongs and broods upon himself as the centre of an epical event and this form progresses till the centre of emotional gravity is equidistant from the artist himself and from others. The narrative is no longer purely personal. The personality of the artist passes into the narration itself, flowing round and round the persons and the action like a vital sea. . . . The dramatic form is reached when the vitality which has flowed and eddied round each person fills every person with such vital force that he or she assumes a proper and intangible esthetic life. . . . The mystery of esthetic like that of material creation is accomplished. [214–215]

"The Structure of the Portrait.*" (Editor's title.) From "The Growth of Imagination" in* James Joyce, *by Richard Ellmann (New York: Oxford University Press, Inc., 1959), pp. 306–9. Copyright © 1959 by Richard Ellmann. Reprinted by permission of Oxford University Press, Inc. All footnotes have been omitted with the permission of the author and the publisher.*

This creator is not male but female; Joyce goes on to borrow an image of Flaubert by calling him a 'god,' but he is really a goddess. Within this womb creatures come to life. No male intercession is necessary even; as Stephen says, 'In the virgin womb of the imagination the word was made flesh.'

Joyce did not take up such metaphors lightly. His brother records that in the first draft of *A Portrait,* Joyce thought of a man's character as developing 'from an embryo' with constant traits. Joyce acted upon this theory with his characteristic thoroughness, and his subsequent interest in the process of gestation, as conveyed to Stanislaus during Nora's first pregnancy, expressed a concern that was literary as well as anatomical. His decision to rewrite *Stephen Hero* as *A Portrait* in five chapters occurred appropriately just after Lucia's birth. For *A Portrait of the Artist as a Young Man* is in fact the gestation of a soul, and in the metaphor Joyce found his new principle of order. The book begins with Stephen's father and, just before the ending, it depicts the hero's severance from his mother. From the start the soul is surrounded by liquids, urine, slime, seawater, amniotic tides, 'drops of water' (as Joyce says at the end of the first chapter) 'falling softly in the brimming bowl.' The atmosphere of biological struggle is necessarily dark and melancholy until the light of life is glimpsed. In the first chapter the foetal soul is for a few pages only slightly individualized, the organism responds only to the most primitive sensory impressions, then the heart forms and musters its affections, the being struggles toward some unspecified, uncomprehended culmination, it is flooded in ways it cannot understand or control, it gropes wordlessly toward sexual differentiation. In the third chapter shame floods Stephen's whole body as conscience develops; the lower bestial nature is put by. Then at the end of the fourth chapter the soul discovers the goal towards which it has been mysteriously proceeding—the goal of life. It must swim no more but emerge into air, the new metaphor being flight. The final chapter shows the soul, already fully developed, fattening itself for its journey until at last it is ready to leave. In the last few pages of the book, Stephen's diary, the soul is released from its confinement, its individuality is complete, and the style shifts with savage abruptness.

The sense of the soul's development as like that of an embryo not only helped Joyce to the book's imagery, but also encouraged him to work and rework the original elements in the process of gestation. Stephen's growth proceeds in waves, in accretions of flesh, in particularization of needs and desires, around and around but always ultimately forward. The episodic framework of *Stephen Hero* was renounced in favor of a group of scenes radiating backwards and forwards. In the new first chapter Joyce had three clusters of sensations: his earliest memories of infancy, his sickness at Clongowes (probably indebted like the ending of 'The Dead' to rheumatic fever in

Trieste), and his pandying at Father Daly's hands. Under these he subsumed chains of related moments, with the effect of three fleshings in time rather than of a linear succession of events. The sequence became primarily one of layers rather than of years.

In this process other human beings are not allowed much existence except as influences upon the soul's development or features of it. The same figures appear and reappear, the schoolboy Heron for example, each time in an altered way to suggest growth in the soul's view of them. Eileen Vance, a partner in childhood games, becomes the object of Stephen's adolescent love poems; the master at Clongowes reappears as the preacher of the sermons at Belvedere. The same words, 'Apologise,' 'admit,' 'maroon,' 'green,' 'cold,' 'warm,' 'wet,' and the like, keep recurring with new implications. The book moves from rudimentary meanings to more complex ones, as in the conceptions of the call and the fall. Stephen, in the first chapter fascinated by unformed images, is next summoned by the flesh and then by the church, the second chapter ending with a prostitute's lingual kiss, the third with his reception of the Host upon his tongue. The soul that has been enraptured by body in the second chapter and by spirit in the third (both depicted in sensory images) then hears the call of art and life, which encompass both without bowing before either, in the fourth chapter; the process is virtually complete. Similarly the fall into sin, at first a terror, gradually becomes an essential part of the discovery of self and life.

Now Stephen, his character still recomposing the same elements, leaves the Catholic priesthood behind him to become 'a priest of eternal imagination, transmuting the daily bread of experience into the radiant body of everlasting life.' Having listened to sermons on ugliness in the third chapter, he makes his own sermons on beauty in the last. The Virgin is transformed into the girl wading on the strand, symbolizing a more tangible reality. In the last two chapters, to suit his new structure, Joyce minimizes Stephen's physical life to show the dominance of his mind, which has accepted but subordinated physical things. The soul is ready now, it throws off its sense of imprisonment, its melancholy, its no longer tolerable conditions of lower existence, to be born.

A Portrait of the Artist as a Young Man: Motif as Motivation and Structure

by Lee T. Lemon

We all know that the subject of *A Portrait of the Artist as a Young Man* is the development of a young man from creature to creator. We can, if we like, push further and point out that the young man develops by casting off the shackles of patriotism, religion, and language. We can further, if we want, talk about the agony of the artist, his sensitivity, his passion, his superciliousness, his necessary irresponsibility, his strugglings to raise himself above his companions— all these and more are part of the complex subject of *A Portrait of the Artist,* and critics have dutifully discussed them.

Critics have also discussed the oddities of the structure of *A Portrait,* justifying the inclusion of baby-talk, sermons, wet-dreams, bulls, and what have you by linking them up with the ages of man, archetypes, mythology, Joyce's Dublin, and Thomistic aesthetics. The usual procedure, when discussion of details has remained inside the novel rather than moving off to other areas, has been to point at numerous instances of whatever detail the critic is specializing in at that moment; the implicit or explicit assumption is that to show repetition is to demonstrate formal value. I should like to go beyond this, to argue that the real theme of *A Portrait* grows from Joyce's peculiar way of handling extremely minute elements, of particles of composition that we will call *motifs.* To the best of my knowledge, *A Portrait* is the first novel in which so much depends upon so little.

Although it is probably well to use *motif* to apply to any element that an author puts into his work (bits of description, statements of characters, props, "stage instructions," and so on), I am interested here only in repeated motifs.[1] A motif may be symbolic, but it is not

[1] Much of the following is based on the analyses of the structure of fiction made about 1920 by the Russian Formalists, especially by Victor Shklovsky and Boris Tomashevsky. See Lee T. Lemon and Marion J. Reis, *Russian Formalist Criticism* (Lincoln, Nebr.: University of Nebraska Press, 1965) for the theoretical background.

strictly a symbol, and a word about the distinction may be helpful. A symbol, I take it, brings the specific quality of its meaning from outside the work. When Burns writes "My luve is like a red, red rose" he is relying upon centuries of convention—the basis of the convention is not important here—dealing with *red* and with *rose*. Although the precise difference might be difficult to specify, we have inherited in our culture a sense that a rose does not suggest quite the same qualities as a petunia, and that a red rose suggests qualities different from those of a white rose. And if I write a novel about a Christopher Passion who dies when he is thirty-three, I am probably importing some meaning from outside the work.

There are, however, numerous details, especially in modern works, which suggest qualities or a tone with a minimum of imported suggestiveness; or, if the detail usually carries a connotation with it, it is used so as to specify an area of suggestion wholly contingent upon the context. The textbooks tell us that rain, for example, is a symbol of fertility; yet in *A Farewell to Arms* it is used to symbolize the sodden gloom, the barrenness, of the world. Hemingway uses it as an objective correlative to give substance to the fears of Catherine and the pessimism of Frederick. I do not want to imply that there is a clear and hard distinction between symbol and motif, but rather to point out that a context may invest qualitatively neutral terms with a richly significant coloration, and qualitatively meaningful terms with unusual meanings. The meaning of a motif, then, is a function of the context; and, to make the whole thing neatly circular, the context is a function of the motifs that make it up.

Although this is the normal condition of literature—most critics of whatever period would admit that details are important—I want to argue that *A Portrait* is the first novel in which motifs *per se* are of primary importance, the first novel in which both theme and structure depend upon such minor elements. In the pre-Joyce novel, the brunt of the meaning is usually carried by the grosser elements, the most important of which is perhaps the fates of the characters. When Pamela marries richly or the Mayor of Casterbridge dies poor, we have a dramatization of the theme that virtue pays and sin suffers. Even so skillful a craftsman as Jane Austen dramatizes the theme of *Pride and Prejudice* by the marital meeting out of perfect poetic justice. Other "gross" ways of making certain that a reader does not miss the theme include authorial intrusions, the "Clarissa" or voice-of-reason character, the interpolated sermon or exemplary set piece, foils to the central characters, and so on. More often than not, an author makes the obviousness of his theme even more obvious by combining several such methods. In the pre-Joyce novel the motif, in so far as it is meaningful, chiefly corroborates what we know through other, more obvious, means.

To get to specifics, *Pride and Prejudice* is about an intelligent, attractive young girl of marriageable age who meets a wealthy, attractive bachelor; the marriage is delayed while she overcomes her prejudices and he overcomes his pride. Their marriage, though, is a natural; all the motifs centering around Darcy and Elizabeth simply support the main action, Jane Austen's clearly implied feelings about marriage, and so on. But if we look at another choice, Stephen's decision not to become a Jesuit, we shall see the difference. It is necessary to quote at length:

> The director stood in the embrasure of the window, his back to the light, leaning an elbow on the brown crossblind and, as he spoke and smiled, slowly dangling and looping the cord of the other blind. Stephen stood before him, following for a moment with his eyes the waning of the long summer daylight above the roofs or the slow deft movements of the priestly fingers. The priest's face was in total shadow but the waning daylight from behind him touched the deeply grooved temples and the curves of the skull. Stephen followed also with his ears the accents and intervals of the priest's voice as he spoke gravely and cordially of indifferent themes. . . . [153–154]

As the priest talks, Stephen remembers "wishing that some unforeseen cause might prevent the director from coming" and then hearing "the handle of the door turning and the swish of a soutane." The priest ridicules *"les jupes"* worn by Franciscans in Belgium and a flame kindles on Stephen's cheek because "the names of articles of dress worn by women or of certain soft and delicate stuffs used in their making brought always to his mind a delicate and sinful perfume." As the priest continues, his eyes search Stephen's face, and Stephen thinks of Jesuits as "men who washed their bodies briskly with cold water and wore clean cold linen." He also remembers being pandied, and a priest talking about Victor Hugo as a heretic. Stephen imagines himself as a seminarian as some Jesuits walk around the cycletrack in the company of ladies. The priest, asking Stephen if he wants to join the order, "let the blindcord fall to one side and, uniting his hands, leaned his chin gravely upon them, communing with himself."

The priest, in effect, has offered Stephen power, knowledge, and the possibility of a life of sinless chastity. Now, all of this is precisely what Stephen has been searching for. He has lived through the sexual shame of adolescence and fought intensely for his purity, he has been professionally engaged as a student in the business of acquiring knowledge, and as a developing artist he requires the power of magical transformation akin to the making of bread and wine into the body and blood of Christ. There is, in short, no apparent reason for refusing the invitation to become a Jesuit; it is the right choice in the eyes of society, family, peers, and Stephen's own conscious self.

Stephen's position here is analogous to that of Elizabeth in *Pride and Prejudice* when Darcy proposes for the first time and she refuses. Here is a summary of Austen's scene: Elizabeth is visiting the Collinses and, while strolling in the nearby park, unexpectedly meets Colonel Fitzwilliam, who rather obliquely informs her that he cannot afford to marry her. As their conversation continues, Elizabeth learns that Darcy, whom she dislikes, prevented an advantageous marriage for her sister Jane, and that Darcy has further seemed to boast of his interference. The result for Elizabeth is agitation, tears, and a headache. Several hours and three paragraphs later, Darcy proposes to Elizabeth and Elizabeth refuses; her decision (though she will reverse it later and though the marriage is desirable from all points of view) grows directly out of the action, out of the large-scale or gross elements that make up the novel.

Stephen's choice is not motivated by such gross considerations. Joyce seems to be saying that Stephen refuses because the priest called attention to his own hands, because Jesuits wash in cold water, because once a priest belittled Hugo, because the priest's eyes were the eyes of a skull, because after the invitation "he smelt again the warm moist air which hung in the bath in Clongowes above the sluggish turfcoloured water" (161), because he thinks of the title The Reverend Stephen Dedalus, S.J., with a sensation of "pallid brick" redness (161). By the end of the chapter, Stephen has accepted his kinship with the "hawklike man flying sunward above the sea" (169) and is revelling in a flood of sensation. What we are actually dealing with in this contrast between the conventional novel and *A Portrait* is the nature of human motivation. Jane Austen seems to say that we base our decisions upon the most immediate and most powerful stimuli touching us. Joyce, on the contrary, shows Stephen deciding on the basis of exceedingly remote and apparently inconsequential stimuli.

Yet the stimuli are not really so inconsequential. Stephen's reaction to the priest's hands, for example, has been carefully prepared for. The preparation, in fact, starts on page 8, when we are told that "Nasty Roche had big hands"; Roche then taunts Stephen about his father. On the next page Stephen's hands are blue with cold, and his parents' hands wave goodbye to him. The prefect's hands impress Stephen as cold and damp, and "that was the way a rat felt, slimy and damp and cold" (22). Stephen is also impressed by Casey's and Eileen's hands, but even though he likes both of them, they are partly objects of fear—Casey because his anti-clericism has made him the object of Dante's hatred and Eileen because she is a Protestant and Dante has told him that to love her is to suffer eternal punishment. The effeminate Tusker Boyle constantly pares his nails, and Gleeson has effeminate hands. The preparation reaches its climax when the prefect of studies cruelly beats Stephen across the hands. I could, of course, trace this motif further into *A Portrait,* but it should already be apparent that Joyce has invested the hands motif with an especially unpleasant quality.

Such is Joyce's artistry that his motifs constantly interweave. The hand motif is closely associated with the motif of punishment, which is in turn even more closely associated with the sight-eye motif. The punishment motif, like all the major motifs in *A Portrait,* begins almost immediately. On page 8 Dante threatens that if Stephen marries Eileen, "the eagles will come and pull out his eyes," which is metamorphosed into the chant:

> Pull out his eyes,
> Apologise,
> Apologise,
> Pull out his eyes.

The reward of sin without repentance is blindness (the priest, remember, toys with the drawstring of a crossblind). Immediately after the chant, Stephen, playing ball, sees the ball through "weak and watery eyes" as a "greasy leather orb [that] flew like a heavy bird through the grey light." When his playmates ask him whether he kisses his mother, he blushes "under their eyes." Later, during an argument about religion and clericism conducted over a turkey (a real bird but also slang for pandybat), Stephen's father exclaims to Dante, "Pity the poor blind" (30). Later in the same argument, Mr. Casey, the anticleric, tells how he routed an old woman who had been harassing him by spitting tobacco juice into her eye and blinding her. At the end of the argument, Casey is first blinded by rage, then his eyes flame, and then he and Stephen's father are blinded by tears. Back at school, Stephen breaks his glasses (blinding himself), and is beaten because he cannot do an assignment. After the beating, "scalding tears" (50) fall from his eyes. When Stephen goes to seek justice, it is through a "dark and silent" corridor, "and his eyes were weak and tired with tears so that he could not see" (55). When he arrives at the rector's desk, there is a skull (the prefect's face, when he issues the invitation, is like a skull). Stephen gets justice, he thinks, only to find that the Jesuits had treated the whole incident as an amusing little joke. When Stephen leaves the rector, he notices his "cool, moist palm" (58).

I shall note only a few more of the references to eyes and punishment; the purpose is not to make a complete list, but rather to show how pervasive such references are. A boy from the street tries to look at a pin-up of Mabel Hunter and complains that he cannot see (67); just before Stephen learns that he has been betrayed by the rector, his father "screwed his glass into his eye and stared hard at both his sons" (72). When Stephen fornicates for the first time, his

eyes, "delighted" just moments before, close when the message in the
"frank uplifted eyes" of the prostitute is "too much for him" (101).
And finally, to keep this from growing endless, there is Heron, with
the face and name of a bird and "a thin hooked nose [which] stood
out between the closeset prominent eyes which were light and in-
expressive" (76). Heron, as Joyce has Stephen remember, is a kind
of minor eagle who will pull out Stephen's eyes if he does not
apologize; Heron's first act is to repeat "Admit" as he lashes Stephen
across the legs (77–78). The scene is repeated several pages later, and
Stephen is left "half blinded with tears . . . clenching his fists madly
and sobbing." On the next page Heron, the avenger, says, "Will you
tell Doyle with my best compliments that I damned his eyes?" (83).

In the crucial invitation scene, it is probably significant that it is
the priest who stands in darkness, who is associated with the "blind,"
whose face is like a skull and so presumably sightless, who stands in
shadow in the sunset. Two things of importance are happening here.
The first, the one I have been discussing, is simply that the images of
sightlessness which surround the priest (along with the emphasis on
his hands and other elements—like coldness and wetness—that I have
not discussed) remind Stephen of his past unpleasant experiences with
priests. As if to drive home the point, Joyce even has Stephen recall
the beatings and badgerings he has taken. These motifs, then, are
both Stephen's motivation for and Joyce's explanation of Stephen's
rejection of the priesthood. Yet they also work in this scene to show
that now, for perhaps the first time in *A Portrait*, Stephen is gaining
a certain control of himself and of his environment. In the past, for
example, the cold, clammy hands were objects of fear; here Stephen
simply notes them. But more important, it is the priest and not
Stephen who is in darkness. Up to this point, Stephen has been literally
or figuratively blinded—with tears, with loss of glasses, with closed
eyes, and so on—in his most crucial moments. In this decisive scene,
Stephen sees—he sees despite his awareness of his previous sins, despite
the audacity of thinking that he might reject the priesthood. Or, to
put the matter differently, he remembers his sins, contemplates a rejection of the Church, and neither apologizes nor is struck blind; Dante's
prophesy, which has been rigorously fulfilled on every similar occasion,
is not fulfilled here.

Stephen decides not to become a priest, in fact, because he *does*
see. He realizes, however faintly, that he will reject the clerical life as
soon as he contrasts his vision of a group of vital young men with
that of the priest's face, "a mirthless reflection of the sunken day."
He tries to imagine himself as a Jesuit and "his name in that new
life leaped into characters before his eyes," eventually becoming a
vision of his own face, "*eyeless* and sourfavoured and devout" (161,

italics mine). He later turns "his eyes coldly for an instant towards the faded blue shrine of the Blessed Virgin which stood fowlwise on a pole." In a moment of doubt later at the University, Stephen tries to "hide his face from their eyes by gazing down sideways into the shallow swirling water under the bridge," (166) but the result is a bit of a poem heavily laden with visual imagery rather than blindness or tears. Stephen both sees and uses his sight. In fact, much of the chapter after the invitation is a paean to sight.

Stephen's full self-realization begins with a mock-baptism that he approaches with "a faint click at his heart, a faint throb in his throat [that] told him once more of how his flesh dreaded the cold infrahuman odour of the sea" (167). But instead of running, Stephen continues walking towards the sea, for somehow, he has changed; the younger Stephen, teased by the boys and threatened with a ducking, would have been blinded by tears. The new Stephen parries "their banter with easy words. How characterless they looked." And although the now proud Stephen finds them repugnant, he is flattered by their attention. The eagle which was to pluck out his eyes, the Heron who playfully lashed Stephen until he admitted, are gone—or rather, like the formerly hateful water, they are transformed. The birds no longer punish, for Stephen has become the bird, the "hawklike man flying sunward above the sea . . . a symbol of the artist forging anew in his workshop out of the sluggish matter of the earth a new soaring impalpable imperishable being" (169). In a beautiful paragraph which mingles latent and overt bird imagery, Stephen's motion is described:

> His heart trembled; his breath came faster and a wild spirit passed over his limbs as though he were soaring sunward. His heart trembled in an ecstasy of fear and his soul was in flight. His soul was soaring in an air beyond the world and the body he knew was purified in a breath and delivered of incertitude and made radiant and commingled with the element of the spirit. An ecstasy of flight made radiant his eyes and wild his breath and tremulous and wild and radiant his windswept limbs. (169)

In such a mood the mock baptism takes place, and Stephen's throat aches "with a desire to cry aloud, the cry of a hawk or eagle on high," for he knows that he will "create proudly out of the freedom and power of his soul, as the great artificer whose name he bore, a living thing, new and soaring and beautiful, impalpable, imperishable" (169–170).

He now joyfully wades in the water he had previously dreaded. The immediate reward of his baptism is a vision and, strangely enough, a vision of a girl described almost as a bird:

> She seemed like one whom magic had changed into the likeness of a strange and beautiful seabird. Her long slender bare legs were delicate as a crane's and pure save where an emerald trail of seaweed had

fashioned itself as a sign upon the flesh. Her thighs, fuller and softhued as ivory, were bared almost to the hips where the white fringes of her drawers were like featherings of soft white down. Her slateblue skirts were kilted boldly about her waist and dovetailed behind her. Her bosom was as a bird's soft and slight, slight and soft as the breast of some darkplumaged dove. But her long fair hair was girlish: and girlish, and touched with the wonder [of] mortal beauty, her face.

She was alone and still, gazing out to sea; and when she felt his presence and the worship of his eyes her eyes turned to him in quiet sufferance of his gaze, without shame or wantonness. Long, long she suffered his gaze and then quietly withdrew her eyes from his. . . .

—Heavenly God! cried Stephen's soul, in an outburst of profane joy. (171)

And thus the change in Stephen is completed; or, more precisely, he has found his direction.

The curious thing about the technique here, and I think the source of a major portion of the structural unity in *A Portrait*, is the fact that the same motifs are used throughout—both before and after Stephen's decision not to become a priest. I shall say more about this later, but now I want to note an important thematic function of this handling of the motifs. I am oversimplifying somewhat, but before the decision and the mock baptism, Stephen's actions are derivative rather than creative. Or, to state this more generally, his experiencing of his own experience has been totally conditioned by the persons, things, and events around him. In the first half of *A Portrait* birds and flying objects are unpleasant because they are seen as variants of Dante's eagle, waiting to swoop down and blind Stephen for any transgression. And (perhaps a partial oversimplification), because Stephen expects to be blinded for his transgressions, he actually is— on numerous occasions. Dante's curse, as it were, is removed only when Stephen literally "sees" birds and girls and everything else with his own eyes. And, of course, the ability to see in its largest sense, to experience freely and accurately and directly, is absolutely necessary if Stephen is to become the kind of artist he wishes to be.

The quality of Stephen's change can perhaps best be shown by contrasting his relationships with Heron and Cranly, both of whom are bird figures. Heron we have already met; Cranly is the avenging priest bird with "the face of a severed head or deathmask. . . . It was a priestlike face, priestlike in its pallor, in the widewinged nose, in the shadowings below the eyes and along the jaws, priestlike in the lips that were long and bloodless and faintly smiling" (178). Now, in the earlier scenes, Heron had the power to intimidate Stephen; Cranly, from the very first, lacks that power. In fact, in the first major dramatized scene between Stephen and Cranly, it is Stephen who takes the initiative, who speaks with "scorn and anger" (194). In the scene immediately following, Stephen is rightfully accused of not being punctual; he again takes the initiative, his eyes "smiling." In the argument about Stephen's refusal to sign the patriotic petition—a return of the apologize motif—Stephen not only does not recant, he turns on the patriot Davin "with cold violence." And in the scene immediately following that, when Stephen's views on art are challenged by the hedonist Lynch, "Stephen turned towards his companion and looked at him for a moment boldly in the eyes. Lynch, recovering from his laughter, answered his look from his humbled eyes" (205).

Near the end of the *Portrait*, Stephen insists upon speaking to Cranly; as they leave the group of boys, they hear the birdcall from *Siegfried*. The ensuing scene is a duel of wits, with Cranly taking up the Dante-Heron apologize-admit motif. Stephen, speaking of his religious feelings, says "I will not serve" (239); Cranly reminds him that his words are satanic, then plies him with questions—do you or don't you believe in the eucharist, how strong are your doubts, and so on. Curiously, Cranly, not Stephen, is embarrassed. In trying to win Stephen back to the Church, Cranly pulls out all the stops, reminding Stephen that he may be condemned to Hell (and Stephen reminds Cranly that the alternative is "an eternity of bliss in the company of the dean of studies"), reminding Stephen that his mind is so "supersaturated" with the religion he professes to disbelieve that he will never escape it, that his lack of faith will break his mother's heart, that his current condition is a result of his environment, of his ultimate uncertainty, and finally that many of the believers share Stephen's doubts. The conversation ends with Stephen in full control:

> I do not fear to be alone or to be spurned for another or to leave whatever I have to leave. And I am not afraid to make a mistake, even a great mistake, a lifelong mistake and perhaps as long as eternity too. . . .
> —Alone, quite alone. You have no fear of that. And you know what that word means? Not only to be separate from all others but to have not even one friend.—I will take the risk, said Stephen.
> —And not to have any one person, Cranly said, who would be more than a friend. . . . (247)

Stephen does not blush, is not blinded by tears at this threat; instead he sees, he sees that Cranly is speaking of his own loneliness.

The final reference to the eyes-punishment cluster of motifs occurs after Stephen has consciously declared his freedom. The April 14 entry in his diary tells of an old man Mulrennan met in the west of Ireland. Stephen comments: "I fear him. I fear his redrimmed horny eyes. It is with him I must struggle all through this night till day come, till he or I lie dead, gripping him by the sinewy throat till. . . . Till what? Till he yield to me? No. I mean him no harm" (252). This is not

the mocking Stephen who argued with Cranly; it is a Stephen who is
too proud to be demoralized by Old Ireland and too much in control
of himself to be vindictive. Stephen has risen above both extremes
and is, we feel, ready to begin his new life.

The quality of the change, I should repeat, is not shown primarily
by overt action on Stephen's part, as it would be in the conventional
novel. It is shown consistently through Joyce's preparation and transformation of a set of motifs.

I have thus far oversimplified by treating Joyce's handling of
motifs as if they were relatively unambiguous—changing, but unambiguous. Actually, one of the lessons Stephen has to learn is that
they are ambiguous, and that the job of the artist is to create a stable
meaning out of the raw flux of reality. In a sense, I have been dealing
with this theme all along, for as I noted earlier, Stephen starts to
become the kind of person he must be only when he denies the
interpretation of reality (birds, for example, and sex and punishment) given by Dante and the Church, and sees these through his
own imagination. Art, to refer this to Stephen's own aesthetic theory,
is the job of creating, of making a vision for contemplation.

Of the numerous instances of such ambiguity towards things or
motifs, I shall cite only a few from the opening pages. One of Stephen's first lessons is that Eileen (the Protestant girl) is both desirable
and dangerous: from his point of view, she is desirable, from Dante's,
a danger to Stephen's soul. Eileen's hands are cold and white when
she puts them over Stephen's eyes. Although this act symbolically
blinds him, its result is illumination of the meaning of the phrase
"Tower of Ivory." As Stephen learns, "By thinking of things you
could understand them" (43). In our terms, Stephen begins to
understand only when his mind begins imposing its own forms upon
things.

Throughout the early pages, Stephen constantly tries to interpret
reality, to make sense of the motifs with which Joyce surrounds him.
He wonders about the multiple meanings of "suck," "belt," "turkey,"
of red and white roses, and so on. The world, for the young Stephen,
is a place where things seem to happen and the fascination of life
consists of trying to make sense out of the relationships between what
seem to be discrete events. That the older Stephen, although he is
not yet fully mature at the end of *A Portrait,* is more certain that
he can impose his vision is perhaps best shown by his poem. The
material of the poem is the motifs that have been used previously—
sexual ardour, eyes, flame, smoke, the transformation of the Eucharist,
sacrificing hands, etc. Stephen, now on his way to maturity, is able
to shape these into a meaningful form. His earlier idle speculation
about the relation of the real girl to the Virgin Mary is now replaced by the creation of his vision of that relationship. We do not,

I think, have to be drawn into the quarrel about the merits of the poem; it is precisely what it is supposed to be—a poem by a young artist and, more importantly, proof that Stephen is the creator and master of his vision.

Yet this portrait of the artist as creator and master of his imagination seems, on first thought, to contradict the explicit aesthetic theory Stephen argues, for his theory of beauty, especially in the context of Thomist aesthetics, is objective; that is, the artist is a discoverer of the beauty intrinsic in things rather than a master of their appearances. Strictly speaking, Stephen seems to hold an imitative theory basing beauty on the recognition of the quiddity or whatness of an object (212–13). But we must also remember that when Stephen discusses Thomas Aquinas' definition, "beauty is that which pleases the senses," he stresses the "pleases" fully as much as he stresses the "that." "Beauty is beheld by the *imagination* which is appeased by the most *satisfying* relations of the sensible" and "all people who admire a beautiful object find in it certain relations which *satisfy* and coincide with the stages themselves of all esthetic apprehension" (208–209, italics mine). Thus even in Stephen's explicit theory there is an important element of subjectivity.

The element of subjectivity—I am not certain that *subjectivity* is the right word; it means here merely a personal and variable relationship between an individual and an object—is even more significant in the creation of beauty than it is in the perception of beauty. Although Stephen calls the final stage of his aesthetic "impersonal," he speaks of the aesthetic images not as being discovered in the thing, but rather as being "conceived in his [the artist's] imagination" (213). And although the artist "refines himself out of existence" he does not take what would seem to be the only other alternative, the objective representation of life, for "the aesthetic image in the dramatic form is life *purified* in and *re*projected from the human imagination" (215, italics mine).

If this incomplete reading of the aesthetic is correct (and I believe it is at least plausible), it helps explain the peculiar rightness of Joyce's choice to show Stephen's development in terms of motifs rather than in terms of grosser kinds of motivation. As a young artist, Stephen's first task is to learn to apprehend for himself the nature of things. He must see them as an individual, not as he has been told they are by Dante, by the priests, by his youthful tormentors. And since beauty is not merely the perception of things or of motifs, but the perception of relationships, he must also learn to see things in a kind of harmony. His youthful blindness is not, in these terms, so much a punishment imposed by Dante and the various symbols of authority as it is a punishment resulting from his faulty perception of things and his consequent inability to relate them harmoniously. He senses, for example, that Eileen is "good," at least for him, although he is told by Dante that she is dangerous; the result is confusion, which is both a kind of blindness and a kind of disharmony. His confusion about whether hands are good or bad, about the emotional tone of coldness, about the pandy-turkey, about moisture, and so on, are part of the same confusion between the qualities of reality he instinctively senses and those he has been taught to respond to. Stephen's freedom begins only when he drifts away from the attitude towards things that had been drilled into him by Dante and the others.

Joyce's handling of motifs, then, not only unifies *A Portrait* but also shows both the motivation for Stephen's change from a sensitive boy besieged by a hostile world to a young man in control of his environment and the peculiar qualities of mind Joyce felt the young artist must possess.

The Artist and the Rose

by Barbara Seward

To even the casual reader of James Joyce it must soon become apparent that the rose is a recurrent symbol in both *A Portrait of the Artist as a Young Man* and *Ulysses*. Its central importance in *Ulysses* as a symbol of Molly Bloom has been adequately demonstrated,[1] and the interrelationship between the *Portrait* and *Ulysses* is universally acknowledged. It is therefore surprising that no one has yet seen fit to examine the flower's complex function in the earlier novel. Taking a place beside water and birds as one of the *Portrait*'s leading symbols, the rose plays a far from negligible role in the development of both structure and theme. Roses blossom at crucial stages of Stephen Dedalus's experience in association with three of his principal concerns: women, religion, and art. Since his conceptions of all three are ambivalent and inseparable, the use of a symbol capable of suggesting various levels of conscious and unconscious meaning is essential to the full expression of his emotional state. Beyond this, his emotional state itself is dynamic and fluctuating, so that the rose takes on additional significance in conveying vital changes in attitudes and reactions determining Stephen's course on the road to maturity.

Joyce, as we know, saw analogies everywhere. In choosing the rose as a dominant symbol for Stephen's intricate emotions, he was choosing a symbol admirably suited to suggesting a complex of these analogies. For centuries the rose has served as emblem of many of man's fundamental concerns, among them those concerns most significant to Stephen. As the flower of beautiful women, it has long been allied with both sensual and spiritual love; and association with the beauty of women is but a short step from association of the rose with the beauty of art. Further, Joyce, who was impressed by such symbolic achievements as the four-fold allegory of Dante's *Comedy* or the indefinite suggestiveness of the early Yeats, could find in these precursors conspicuous roses used as symbols of women, religion, and art. With

---

"*The Artist and the Rose*" by Barbara Seward. *From* University of Toronto Quarterly, *XXVI (January, 1947), 180–90. Copyright 1947 by the University of Toronto. Reprinted by permission of the University of Toronto Press.*

[1] William York Tindall, "Dante and Mrs. Bloom," *Accent*, XI (Spring, 1951), 85–92.

traditional analogies supporting and enhancing private preoccupations, he was able to enrich Stephen's rose by introducing evocations of objective beliefs into the interplay of subtle subjective impressions.

The symbol's association with Stephen is made on the very first page of the *Portrait*. This in itself is surely an indication of its intended importance; for Joyce, who was notably exacting about every word and the position of every word in his books, was anything but negligent of his opening pages. Here Stephen learns a song about a rose:

> *Oh, the wild rose blossoms*
> *On the little green place.*
> He sang that song. That was his song.
> *Oh, the green wothe botheth.* [7]

The little green place clearly suggests Ireland, while the wild rose hardly less clearly suggests Stephen, who is at this time in the blossoming stage, who specifically claims the song as "his," and who is to be essentially rebellious, alone, and in his own terms "wild" throughout his Irish youth. With the green rose in the child's own version of the song, hints of Stephen's artistic inclinations are introduced. By altering the wording he is exercising incipient creativity, and by positing a green rose he is creating in imagination that which does not exist elsewhere. As a flower whose colour is that of Ireland and whose creation is dependent upon Stephen's imagination, the green rose of the child's initial artistic effort acts as a symbolic foreshadowing of the young man's final determination "to forge in the smithy of my soul the uncreated conscience of my race." [253]

The green rose also appears to be related to Stephen's emotional condition. Green is suggestive of fertility and therefore of potentiality, but at the same time implies present unripeness or immaturity. In this respect the flower is associated not only with Stephen's youth but also with his persistent desire to discover an impossible, subjective ideal in the actual world. The association is made specific when, during Stephen's first school experience, the War of the Roses in his mathematics class calls his song to mind again [12] : "But you could not have a green rose. But perhaps somewhere in the world you could." And his thought here is simply an early expression of the longing that later dominates his adolescence, "to meet in the real world the unsubstantial image which his soul so constantly beheld." [65]

This interpretation is supported by the fact that Stephen's fantasies of Mercedes, the "unsubstantial image" in question, always have a rose garden for their setting. The ideal of Mercedes was derived from Stephen's reading *The Count of Monte Cristo* and identifying himself with the novel's hero in his love for the girl of that name. In fact, Stephen's fantasy owes to Dumas almost every romantic detail: a lady who embodies all goodness and virtue, a love that will weather untold hardships, and, when his dream shall have been betrayed, a triumph no less glorious than the passion that provokes it. But Stephen's ideal is framed with roses which do not appear in Dumas: "Outside Black-rock, on the road that led to the mountains, stood a small whitewashed house in the garden of which grew many rosebushes: and in this house, he told himself, another Mercedes lived." [62–63] Since no rose garden is to be found in Dumas (although almost all else down to the whitewash is Dumas), Joyce undoubtedly adds it with symbolic intent. Through associating Mercedes with roses he is able to make more evident her relation to other women in the *Portrait* who are also associated with roses. Further, his use of symbolism in the treatment of Mercedes enables him to express more than a single meaning and thus to suggest the complexity of young Stephen's attitude towards women.

The ideal lady in her rose garden is on one level reminiscent of Beatrice, who leads Dante to the rose of heaven and is herself enthroned on one of its petals. Other features of Stephen's fantasy support this association. The Count of Monte Cristo, with whom Stephen identifies himself, is named Edmond Dantès. In addition to the likeness of names, both Dante and Dantès were proud and angry exiles, intense moral idealists, and devoted lovers. In each, love for the lady remained chaste and unconsummated; in each it served as moral guide throughout an otherwise troubled life.[2] Then, reinforcing the clear Dantesque parallels to *The Count of Monte Cristo* (which Joyce, if not Dumas, was surely aware of), are two further parallels to Dante, pointed up by Joycean modifications of Dumas. While Dantès is in his teens at the time of falling in love with Mercedes, Stephen, like Dante, is still a child. More important, while Dantès' Mercedes lives on a promontory, Stephen's lives on a road leading to mountains. The substitution of mountains for promontory seems deliberate: Dante's attempt to climb the holy hill when he lost his way in the dark wood of sense and his success in climbing Purgatory by grace imparted through Beatrice both find their echo in Stephen's later youth when he, lost in his own dark wood, experiences relief in remembering his early vision of purity: [99] "In the pauses of his desire, when the luxury that was wasting him gave room to a softer languor, the image of Mercedes traversed the background of his memory. He saw again the small white house and the garden of rosebushes on the road that led to the mountains."

The association of Mercedes with roses that have perceptible Dan-

---

[2] Dantès, throughout his long career of vengeance, regarded himself as a veritable agent of Providence sent to punish his betrayers. Mercedes, the chief motive behind his fierce justice, was alone able to temper his vengeful excesses when they threatened the life of her innocent son.

tesque hues links her to other rose-women in the *Portrait* who are also in some sense Beatrice-like. Whether secular or spiritual, the later roses have roots in Mercedes' garden, for Stephen's childhood fantasy-woman embodies within herself the seeds of those to follow. First among her descendants is the Virgin herself. As a chaste, ennobling influence Mercedes plays a role in Stephen's consciousness (as does Beatrice in Dante's) which is similar in some ways to that of Mary. During his struggles with lust and guilt, when memories of Mercedes brought transitory balm, the idea of the Virgin was a still more potent source of inspiration and relief. Since the rose is traditionally symbolic of the Virgin as well as of womankind, Stephen's experience of penance as expressed in prayers to Mary is appropriately conveyed by the same flower that has been associated with his earlier female idol: "his prayers ascended to heaven from his purified heart like perfume streaming upwards from a heart of white rose." [145] The use of rose symbolism for both Mary and Mercedes to evoke analogous moods of elevated serenity makes apparent a parallel between Stephen's divine and earthly ideals.

But the correspondence between ideals and roses is devious. While Stephen's conscious worship of chastity at this time is strongly influenced by his unquestioning Catholicism,[3] his unconscious reactions to womankind are not entirely in accord with Catholic ideals. In a novel told entirely from Stephen's conscious point of view, such unconscious reactions must be conveyed primarily by symbolic indirection. The roses of Mercedes and the Virgin indicate Stephen's suppressed sensual desires as well as his acknowledged admiration for holiness. Mercedes' dwelling in a garden of rosebushes, through suggesting the idealized sexuality of the *Roman de la Rose*, clarifies the nature of the "strange unrest" Stephen felt when he "brooded upon her image." [64] And the "heart of white rose" he offers to the Virgin at the end of the religious retreat ironically recalls his sensations at its outset: "Stephen's heart had withered up like a flower of the desert that feels the simoom coming from afar." [108]

Such intimations of unconscious sexual stirrings are reinforced by association with other symbols. Stephen's painful, ascetic attempts to transform the "withered" flower of his sensual nature into the purified "white rose" of the Virgin evoke the novel's recurrent associations of white, the colour of Catholic purity, with cold, dank, unpleasant things.[4] More specifically, the Virgin's flower recalls the only other

---

[3] An unresolved Oedipus complex also seems to be influential. In Freudian theory guilt over unconscious incestuous desires often results in a dichotomizing of women into pure women, placed in the mother category, and women who are sexually attractive but therefore evil.

[4] See Hugh Kenner, "The Portrait in Perspective," [reprinted above, pp. 26–37—Ed.]

white rose in the *Portrait,* that worn by Stephen during the early War of the Roses in his mathematics class. On this occasion Stephen's white rose is defeated by the opposing red rose, just as later his religious ideal of chastity, associated with the Virgin's white rose, was to be defeated by a victorious sensual ideal, associated with the more commonly secular red rose.

Red and white roses, then, symbolize Stephen's conflict between the flesh and the spirit. It is notable that Joyce assigned no colour to the roses surrounding Mercedes, and this is possibly because she is Stephen's "unsubstantial image," the green rose of the child's still undefined longing. Certainly the fantasy of Mercedes contains in embryo both religious and profane poles of Stephen's conflict, while his subsequent worship of the Virgin represents his first conscious choice between opposites. Since the choice is contrary to his nature, his repudiation of the Virgin in favour of a secular ideal is almost inevitable. Significantly, his reversal, the climax of the book, again reminds us of Mercedes and this time culminates in a gigantic red rose.

Through his encounter with the girl on the beach Stephen is converted from the worship of things divine to the worship of things earthly. The significance of this inverted conversion is to a great extent communicated by symbolism which expresses opposition to Catholicism through association with a markedly secular rose. Throughout the experience, Stephen's most frequent adjective is "wild," indicating both rebellion and release, and echoing the "wild rose" with which he identified himself in infancy. The girl, recalling Mercedes, is suggestive of Beatrice: like Beatrice, she has come as a messenger of ultimate truth, and, like Beatrice, she will guide Stephen by her eyes to his vision of ineffable glory. But going beyond Mercedes, the girl on the beach is a now avowedly sensual Beatrice, and the vision to which her inspiration leads will be an avowedly secular vision: "Her eyes had called him and his soul had leaped at the call. . . . A wild angel had appeared to him, the angel of mortal youth and beauty, an envoy from the fair courts of life to throw open before him in an instant of ecstasy the gates of all the ways of error and glory." [172]

Stephen's "instant of ecstasy" follows almost immediately his experience of the girl. He is no longer near her (as Dante was no longer beside Beatrice in his final ecstasy), but "her image had passed into his soul for ever." [172] Lying down upon the beach to calm his agitation, he is granted a vision of a rose of heavenly light which is a temporal image of Dante's rose of God [172]:

His eyelids trembled . . . as if they felt the strange light of some new world . . . fantastic, dim, uncertain as under sea, traversed by cloudy shapes and beings. A world, a glimmer, or a flower? Glimmering and trembling, trembling and unfolding, a breaking light, an opening flower, it spread in endless succession to itself, breaking in full crimson and un-

folding and fading to palest rose, leaf by leaf and wave of light by wave
of light, flooding all the heavens with its soft flushes.

Stephen's ecstasy is brief and Dante's is protracted, so that a thorough
comparison between the two would necessitate a reading of the
Paradiso's last four cantos. Nevertheless, it is possible to gain some
conception of the close parallel (in light, water imagery, shapes and
beings, vast opening flower) from Dante's description of the rose's
initial manifestation to him (XXX, 106–117) :

> *Fassi di raggio tutta sua parvenza*
> *riflesso al sommo del Mobile Primo,* **. . .**
> *E come clivo in acqua di suo imo*
> *si specchia.* . . .
> *sì soprastando al lume intorno intorno*
> *vidi specchiarsi in più di mille soglie,*
> *quanto di noi lassù fatto ha ritorno.*
> *E se l' infimo grado in sè raccoglie*
> *sì grande lume, quant' è la larghezza*
> *di questa rosa nell' estreme foglie?*

Joyce's presentation of Stephen's climactic vision through symbolism strongly reminiscent of the *Paradiso* emphasizes the simultane-
ous opposition and kinship between Stephen's experience and Dante's.
Stephen being inspired by primarily sensual feelings, the crimson rose
represents his supreme affirmation of the "wonder of mortal beauty,"
in direct contrast to Dante's white rose of spiritual beauty. At the
same time the analogy with Dante's rose enhances the tremendous
significance of Stephen's. It is notable that Stephen, like Molly Bloom
and Anna Livia, is granted his moment of supreme affirmation in the
borderland between sleep and waking when the relaxation of the
critical intellect presumably facilitates cosmic insights.[5] His twilight
vision of a Dantesque rose of mortal glory, symbolizing his new comprehension of life's meaning, clearly implies that Stephen's ecstasy has
for him something of the transcendent import that Dante's had for
Dante.

Beneath the experience, however, lurks an ironic undertone that
becomes magnified in retrospect. The immediate effect of Stephen's
conversion to the worship of mortal beauty is his realization of his
true vocation. Dedication to art fills the place left vacant by his repudiation of the priesthood, and after developing an aesthetic theory
applying Thomistic concepts to art for art's sake doctrine, Stephen is
ready to write a poem putting theory into practice. The symbolic

[5] Cf. Yeats's "moment when we are both asleep and awake . . . in which the mind
liberated from the pressure of the will is unfolded in symbols"—*Essays* (New York,
1924), 193; and T. S. Eliot's visionary lady "who moves in the time between sleep-
ing and waking" (*Ash Wednesday*).

atmosphere surrounding the creation of this poem parallels that of his experience on the beach in almost every detail. Again inspired by a girl who is for the moment the centre of Stephen's emotional universe, the poem is composed in a like state of visionary ecstasy expressed by clouds, water, light, and most notably another Dantesque rose. Since this experience is more extensive and complex than its earlier counterpart, a close analysis of the symbolism through which it is conveyed illuminates the real conflict underlying Stephen's attitude and the irony of his ecstatic conviction.

Stephen's second vision simultaneously encompasses the three main levels of meaning associated with the rose: religion, woman, and art. Like its predecessor, it takes place in the borderland between dream and waking and unfolds in cloudlike rays of rosy light [217]:

> Over his limbs in sleep pale cool waves of light had passed. He lay still, as if his soul lay amid cool waters. . . . His mind was waking slowly to a tremulous morning knowledge, a morning inspiration. . . . In a dream or vision he had known the ecstasy of seraphic life. . . . The instant flashed forth like a point of light and now from cloud on cloud of vague circumstance confused form was veiling softly its afterglow . . . deepening to a rose and ardent light.

Here the *Paradiso* is recalled by the imagery of watery light at the outset of Stephen's vision as well as by the emerging rose. Just as Dante's mystic rose of heaven first appeared to him as a river of light (*E vidi lume in forma di riviera: Par.* XXX, 61), so Stephen's second Dantesque rose now evolves from a dreamlike impression of light and waters.[6] The inescapable analogy with Dante is again made partly to mark the comparison between Stephen's experience of mortal beauty and Dante's of heavenly beauty. But as a symbol of specifically creative ecstasy, the rose of the *Paradiso* is still more suggestive. Not only is it the culmination of one of the world's greatest literary creations, but it also symbolizes therein the divine fulfilment of God's eternal creation. Stephen's exalted conception of the artist could scarcely have found more appropriate expression.

As the vision unfolds, further implications for art develop. Stephen's rose, like Dante's, becomes the Virgin's flower. And, in accord with Stephen's customary conversion of spiritual entities to secular uses, the Virgin herself becomes associated with his markedly secular theory of art. The art for art's sake doctrine, already presented explicitly in Stephen's talk with Lynch [204–215], is here presented by symbolic indirection. The Annunciation is made to symbolize artistic inspiration

---

[6] Water here also suggests rebirth, as has Stephen's wading in the first vision. His poem's completion employs similar imagery to indicate his rebirth as artist through acceptance of sex [223]: "Her nakedness . . . enfolded him like water with a liquid life . . . the liquid letters of speech . . . flowed forth over his brain."

[217] : "O! in the virgin womb of the imagination the word was made flesh. Gabriel the seraph had come to the virgin's chamber." And the Annunciation as symbol of poetic inspiration is presently complemented by the Eucharist, symbol of poetic composition [221] : ". . . transmuting the daily bread of experience into the radiant body of everliving life." Following Stephen's aesthetic theory, artistic creation is presented as a dual process in which inspiration first makes the word flesh (i.e., gives rise to an "epiphany" or illuminating insight), and artistic discipline then makes the flesh word (i.e., gives the insight "wholeness, harmony, and radiance," thereby moulding it into an aesthetic form).

It is notable that these concepts, here associated with Dante's flower of heaven and Mary, are again associated with a rose by Stephen's remarks in *Ulysses* [385/391] : "Desire's wind blasts the thorntree but after it becomes from a bramblebush to be a rose upon the rood of time. . . . In woman's womb word is made flesh but in the spirit of the maker all flesh that passes becomes the word that shall not pass away." Stephen, still identifying the artist with the divine Creator, still associates the rose with the process of artistic creation. Although he has now substituted Yeats's "rose upon the rood of time" for Dante's rose of heaven, there is small difference in effect. For Yeats's rose of Eternal Beauty, like Dante's rose of Eternity, symbolizes the beginning and end of art and life; and Yeats, like Dante, believed (or tried to believe) that art was a bodying forth of spiritual mysteries. Joyce, seeking symbolic expression for Stephen's secular aesthetics, continues to choose the most transcendental of literary roses to emphasize the supreme importance to Stephen of his doctrine of earthly beauty in art.

Beauty has become Stephen's highest value in life as well. Since beauty throughout the *Portrait* has been associated with women at least as much as with art, and since the sensual charm of a woman has been directly responsible for Stephen's conversion to mortal beauty, it is not surprising to find yet another woman involved in his creation of a poem. Again the rose as the Virgin's flower is important, and here the opposition to Dante is most strongly marked. Stephen's girl, who has inspired his creative ecstasy, is a virgin and a Catholic, "her life . . . a simple rosary of hours." [216] But in his fantasy she becomes a temptress awakening man's lust, a universal embodiment of all that is opposed to Mary [217–218] :

> That rose and ardent light was her strange wilful heart, strange that no man had known or would know, wilful from before the beginning of the world: and lured by that ardent roselike glow the choirs of the seraphim were falling from heaven. . . . Its rays burned up the world, consumed the hearts of men and angels: the rays from the rose that was her wilful heart.

In the sacrilegious spirit of the *fin de siècle*, this passage recalls the "mystical rose of the mire" of Swinburne's "Dolores" or the "rose that is rooted in hell" of Arthur Symons's "Rosa Flammae." Stephen, still preoccupied with the religion he is repudiating, has used Dantesque imagery to translate his sexual desire into anti-Catholic terms and to create of its object an inverted Virgin who is as potent a force for damnation as Mary is for salvation.

His conceptions of art and woman are, then, at this time inseparable. Both are aesthetic, sensual, and anti-Catholic, and both rest on the same infirm emotional foundation. Two further analogies complement the analogy with Dante in revealing the attitudes underlying Stephen's ecstasy. His idealized rose-woman, existing "from before the beginning of the world" and sending forth rays of beauty that "consumed the hearts of men and angels," echoes Yeats's "Rose of the World," who existed before there were angels "or any hearts to beat" and for whose beauty "Troy passed away in one high funeral gleam." Stephen's rose, like Yeats's, is at once the inspiration of his art, the particular woman to whom he is attracted, and the embodiment of his ideal of beauty; and Stephen, like Yeats, is limited at this stage by highly subjective, romantic, and immature attitudes which he too is later to repudiate. A passage from Joyce's own early essay on James Clarence Mangan completes the picture. Writing of the moving spirit in Mangan's poetry, Joyce describes it as a feminine symbol of ideal beauty, a "flower of flowers" remarkably similar to Yeats's or Stephen's:

> the presence of an imaginative personality reflecting the light of imaginative beauty is . . . vividly felt. . . . Music and odours and lights are spread about her. . . . Vittoria Colonna and Laura and Beatrice . . . embody one chivalrous idea . . . and she whose white and holy hands have the virtue of enchanted hands, his virgin flower, the flower of flowers, is no less than these an embodiment of that idea.[7]

It is significant that this essay was published in *St. Stephen's* for May 1902, a few months before Joyce's winter flight from Dublin and therefore at approximately the time when the autobiographical Stephen was composing his poem.

Despite his elaborate conversion to mortal beauty, Stephen is still in much the same frame of mind as the child who dreamed of a green rose that couldn't exist. He had set out to discover his "unsubstantial" ideal "in the real world," but sought it in Virgin and anti-Virgin, heaven and hell, ironically ignoring the solid earth in between. His adherence to the lush, world-weary romanticism of the 1890's reflects

---

[7] Quoted in Herbert Gorman, *James Joyce* (New York, 1948), 76–77. Joyce borrows "flower of flowers" from Mangan's "Dark Rosaleen," a version of the traditional Irish song, allusions to which are also present in Yeats's rose poems.

the introverted adolescence of his present emotional orientation, while his use of Dante in expressing rebellion against the Church reveals his continuing preoccupation with the religion he has rejected. Turning from the spirit to the flesh, Stephen has simply substituted one side of his conflict for the other without working out a satisfactory resolution. His reaction to woman is now a purely sensual thing and his artistic ideal does not go beyond the aesthete's hollow shell of formal beauty. He himself is dimly conscious of dissatisfaction when, at the very pinnacle of creative ecstasy, inspiration suddenly fails him [221–222]:

> The full morning light had come . . . he knew that all around him life was about to awaken in common noises, hoarse voices, sleepy prayers. Shrinking from that life he turned towards the wall . . . staring at the great overblown scarlet flowers of the tattered wallpaper. . . . Weary! Weary! He too was weary of ardent ways.

But he remains unconscious of the nature of his trouble, also hinted at in this passage. The awakening of daily life causes Stephen's roses to appear "overblown" because he cannot yet come to terms with that life. He is suffering primarily from an egocentricity that excludes charity, and he will achieve neither a true resolution of conflicts nor an adequate conception of art until his discovery of humanity, the subject of *Ulysses*.

A little epiphany towards the close of the *Portrait* illuminates Stephen's condition and serves almost as a forecast of his course in *Ulysses*. The epiphany is associated with a woman who is again a rose. Stephen and Cranly overhear a servant singing "Rosie O'Grady," and in Stephen's mind she is alternately related to each of his unreconciled conceptions of woman, the spiritual and the secular. He first envisions "the figure of woman as she appears in the liturgy of the church" [244], thereby evoking the Beatrice-Virgin-Catholic aura of his earlier rose-women. The image passes and he later thinks of his girl, the rosy temptress of his recent villanelle, whom he now realizes he is losing to Cranly [245]: "Yes; he would go. He could not strive against another. He knew his part." But the singer herself is actually a typical Irish servant, a representative of the ordinary humanity from which egocentric Stephen holds himself aloof.

Cranly, well ahead of Stephen in tolerance and sympathy, unites all these women through the phrase, *"Mulier cantat";* for in their fundamental kinship, which Stephen fails to comprehend, lies a potential resolution of his difficulties. Commenting on the lyrics of "Rosie O'Grady," Cranly attempts to point out to Stephen the charity that is lacking in his cold art and selfish life [244–245]:

> —There's real poetry for you, he said. There's real love.
> He glanced sideways at Stephen with a strange smile and said:

—Do you consider that poetry? Or do you know what the words mean?
—I want to see Rosie first, said Stephen.
—She's easy to find, Cranly said.

But Stephen is not yet ready to understand, can understand only his own isolation. Not until his comprehension of Molly Bloom, the ultimate rose of human life, will he learn what the words love and poetry mean and find his fulfilment "in the real world."

Art and Life: The Aesthetic of the *Portrait*

by S. L. Goldberg

To approach Joyce's art theoretically, through his aesthetic, is not without its dangers. The commonest mistake is to take that aesthetic as a sort of criterion, a point of reference by which to measure Joyce's artistic success. Probably every reader of modern literature has met Stephen Dedalus's theory in the *Portrait* and his views on Shakespeare in *Ulysses*, and it seems only natural to apply Joyce's own aesthetic in the criticism of his books, if not of all literature. The fact is, however, that the real value of the aesthetic theories is of a different kind. For it is always dangerous to judge a writer's work by his own theories —we tend, only too easily, to beg the most relevant questions; and these dangers are particularly acute when, as in Joyce's case, the theories appear as an integral part of a complex work of art. But if they cannot supply us with a critical yardstick, or even a useful structure of the author's intentions, they *can* help us, I believe, in another way: if we are prepared to follow them patiently and critically, they lead us directly towards the preoccupations and the forms of his imagination.

The main interest of the aesthetic theory in the *Portrait* (and in *Ulysses* too) arises from the fact that it brings many of the themes of the novel itself to a convenient focus—in particular, both the kind of attitudes that subtly impel Stephen all through it and the limitations of those attitudes as well. The theory is primarily Stephen's, not Joyce's, even though Joyce used many of his own ideas in it, and to examine it is largely to examine Stephen as a dramatic character. The theory therefore offers a convenient starting-point for critical discussion of the art; yet even while it does so, it offers peculiar difficulties of its own.

One is simply the terminology that Joyce, and Stephen after him, adopted from his reading in Scholastic philosophy, and the rather

elliptical and even crabbed style of his thought: its "scholastic stink",
as one character puts it. This hardly makes for easy understanding or
easy exposition—so much so, indeed, that to approach Joyce's work this
way may seem (I confess) all too like struggling through a hedge
instead of going in by the gate. But there are further difficulties still.
The theory both in the *Portrait* and *Ulysses* raises problems of interpretation which are precisely equivalent to those raised by the novels
themselves and which have no easy solution. No one could claim
that the theory is always clear even when it is most explicit, and what
Joyce has written about aesthetics in various places is still so scrappy
that we can call it a full aesthetic theory only with a generous courtesy.
But to increase the difficulty, it is not always very easy to distinguish
between his own views and those of Stephen Dedalus. Joyce himself
made some jottings on aesthetics in his notebooks in 1903–04; these
are echoed both in *Stephen Hero* and the *Portrait*. He delivered two
papers to his college Literary and Historical Society on "Drama and
Life" (1900) and "James Clarence Mangan" (1902), which are
echoed in *Stephen Hero* and in *Ulysses*.[1] The term "epiphany", which
is mentioned in *Stephen Hero*, not mentioned in the *Portrait* and
then recalled in *Ulysses*, is one the young Joyce is known to have used
himself for tiny sketches. However closely they resemble each other,
none of these theories is exactly the same. Naturally enough, almost
every critic of Joyce's work supports his view of it by an interpretation
of what he takes to be Joyce's own aesthetic, even if the support is
only that of a suggestive analogy; and it is clear that some interpretation at least is required. Yet the very fact that interpretations of the
art and of the theory are so closely linked also requires us to make
sure we view the latter as accurately as the former, and that we understand the full implications both of what Joyce has Stephen say in any
particular context and, equally, of what he does not have him say.
The basic problem of Joyce's aesthetic, in other words, is like that of
his art—to detect where, and how, Joyce qualifies the attitudes of *the
artist as a young man*. Critical probing as well as exposition is called
for.

If we examine these various theories in relation to each other it
quickly appears that those in the novels are more highly wrought,
more developed, than anything that survives of Joyce's personal comments. It is understandable enough that Stephen's remarks in the

[1] The jottings in the notebooks are printed by Herbert Gorman in his *James
Joyce: a Definitive Biography*, London (1941), 1949, the pages of which I have cited
in brackets in the text. They are also reprinted in *The Critical Writings of James
Joyce*, ed. Ellsworth Mason and Richard Ellmann, London, 1959. The latter volume
also includes the two early papers by Joyce (which were used for the essay on "Art
and Life" Stephen delivers to his college Society in *Stephen Hero*), together with
Joyce's other essays and reviews—none of which, however, adds anything much of
general theoretical value.

Portrait should have led to an inflation of their value as a general aesthetic and some not very convincing applications of them to Joyce's work. But even on a casual reading, Stephen's character in the *Portrait* ought to provoke a certain caution about his theories. His emancipation from his society, for example, is clearly less assured than he supposes, and despite his citation of Aquinas in support of his aesthetic, the forms in which his imagination actually expresses itself seem more like those of a late nineteenth-century aesthete than a tough-minded, twentieth-century neo-Thomist. He is obviously not to be identified with the artist as an older man. If we look at Joyce's other novels, moreover, we also notice that Stephen is portrayed with far less irony in *Stephen Hero* and with a far more complex irony in *Ulysses*. This general difference is reflected in the differences between the theories he propounds in each work, differences important not only for their theoretical implications but also for their dramatic implications about the novel in which they appear. In other words, if we put the theory in the *Portrait* side by side with those in the notebooks and Joyce's other writings and *Stephen Hero*, and press certain problems they raise, we can hardly avoid concluding that the theory Stephen advances in the *Portrait* is not a satisfactory aesthetic in itself, that its force in the novel is not so much philosophical as dramatic, and that it awaits completion and rectification by the views he advances in *Ulysses*. The theory in the *Portrait* serves to reveal not so much the nature of art as the nature of Stephen Dedalus; and to miss this, or to attempt to assess Joyce's work by the theory as he there presents it, is inevitably to distort his artistic achievement.

Before examining the theory, however, it is probably as well to clarify right at the start two or three other common assumptions about it and about Joyce's art. The first is that, whatever difficulties we find in Stephen's views, Joyce's *own* theory is all of a piece, and was so from the very beginning, and that to discover what it is, all we need do is simply find the common denominators in his various formulations, supply the assumptions that will reconcile them together, and interpret the result to taste. The second assumption is that this underlying aesthetic is specifically Thomist, or neo-Thomist, and that what Stephen Dedalus says in various places is "correctly" interpreted as what Aquinas meant or what others have since constructed on a foundation of his ideas. Both assumptions are highly questionable. To take only one example: it is true, as any examination of the theories quickly reveals, that the notion of what Joyce called "epiphanies", which is touched on in *Stephen Hero* (but nowhere else, and never explicitly developed), is essential to any aesthetic attributable to Joyce himself. It is also true that the theory in the *Portrait* is crippled by the omission of the concept (or something like it), while the more satisfactory theory in *Ulysses* depends upon it. But the concept as it is assumed in *Ulysses* is rather different from the form in which it is mentioned in *Stephen Hero*, and if we wish to understand Joyce's own views we ought to take that difference into account. We may, for whatever reasons, prefer the early formulation with its vaguely metaphysical flavour (although personally I do not), but we cannot reasonably presume that it represents Joyce's own, real and always consistent view. But the real importance of this is its bearing on the second assumption. Although the notion of "epiphanies" is of central importance, some critics have tried to add it to Joyce's other aesthetic theories by supplying him with a gratuitous metaphysical system, and interpreting "epiphanies", as well as the terms Stephen explicitly borrows from Aquinas, in a fully Scholastic sense. Despite his Scholastic terminology, Joyce's aesthetic is not strictly Thomist at all. Nor is there any real evidence whatever that he gave any of his aesthetic terms a theological meaning, or that he intended at any stage to reveal through art the ordered spiritual vision of Christianity. He may never have cast off the effect of his religion even though he rejected it, or escaped the influence of his Jesuit teachers; on the other hand, his reading in Aquinas seems to have been private and idiosyncratic, and certainly not undertaken in pursuit of a Catholic philosophy. Joyce was never a philosopher of any kind, and we must not read too much into what he actually wrote for the sake of making it consonant with what we perhaps feel he ought to have written.

Another temptation, closely connected with this, is to overemphasize Stephen's theological analogies. In the course of his discussion, both in the *Portrait* and again in *Ulysses*, he compares the artist with God; and though the insights his analogies are designed to illuminate are better postponed until later chapters, it is probably as well to insist at the beginning that his analogies are *only* analogies, not identifications. He is not arguing from art to religion, as is sometimes thought; he is advancing aesthetic doctrines, not metaphysics. When he compares the (limited) autonomy of art and of the human artist to the (unlimited) autonomy of God, we ought not suppose that his metaphor elevates the one to the place of the other or was meant to. Again, if he sometimes uses phrases or doctrines of doubtful religious orthodoxy, this may perhaps shock some people (as no doubt the aggressive young Stephen intended), but it does not necessarily invalidate his point about art. The foundations of his theory do not lie in his theological analogies, which are more expository devices than experiential premises, and we have to ask what purpose they serve, what point Stephen is really making, before assuming that his unorthodoxy is a dramatic hint from Joyce that his character's theory is completely wrong. The difficulty with Stephen's theories, indeed, is that they are not wrong in any simple, black-and-white sense at all; he is always at least partly right. The weaknesses are a matter of his emphasis—what he neglects, what he over-stresses, what he therefore distorts.

At bottom, both Joyce and Stephen are concerned with one main set of aesthetic problems: the relations between art and life, or (in slightly different terms) between the artist-as-man and the artist-as-artist. These are inevitably among the central problems of any aesthetic in our post-Romantic era, and they admit of no easy, universal solution. On the one hand, the desire to dissociate art and life has an obvious motive and an obvious validity—a work of art is not properly the direct expression of social or personal attitudes, and not therefore to be estimated simply as a social or psychological or moral epiphenomenon. It exists in its own right and demands a response in its own terms. On the other hand, the desire to relate art and life is no less necessary and no less valid—a work of art is a human artifact and it necessarily exists in a social context. Looking back over the various attempts of the last century and a half to satisfy these apparently conflicting impulses, we may at least say that either impulse alone is likely to emasculate art or to pervert its integrity unless checked by the motives and insights that prompt the other. The difficulties of the artist himself in coming to terms with a society that all too crudely demands his service or all too easily provokes his rejection—difficulties from which perhaps no significant artist since Blake has been free—serve only to heighten the theoretical confusions. Joyce himself offers a classical example of the issues, and all the more so since he was so conscious of them and tried, in the dramatic figure of Stephen Dedalus, at once to present them and to work out a solution. And although the terms in which he did so can be assessed only in a detailed analysis of his art, these issues constitute the broad underlying significance of Stephen's theorizing, and particularly of the most marked change of emphasis discernible between his views in the *Portrait* and those in *Ulysses*.

In the former novel, Stephen is intent on the dissociation of art and life, on the autonomy and integrity of the work of art in itself. In the course of his argument, however, he conspicuously underestimates the other side of the matter: the positive relations between the work of art and the life from which it springs, which it engages in others, and which it expresses in its own terms. The result is that what he says is largely disabled by what he omits. As it stands, his theory lapses all too readily into a barren formalism encouraging a purely internal analysis of works of art, a concentration on their patterns of organization to the exclusion of questions of imaginative depth and value. (Indeed, to view Joyce's own art through the theory in the *Portrait* would lead to just that kind of formalistic analysis and evasion of judgment it has received from some of its commentators.) Up to a point, Stephen's supplementary theory of aesthetic forms—"lyrical", "epical" and "dramatic"—is an attempt to fill this gap; but in so far as it is, it remains strikingly inconsistent with his more extended, and obviously more personally important, theory of beauty and art. The theory of forms really foreshadows what he attempts in *Ulysses*—and for this reason I have reserved treatment of it until Chapter III and (more thoroughly) Chapter VI: to understand it fully requires a context larger than that provided by the *Portrait* alone. But this being the case, it is also quite clear that the views in *Ulysses* make no complete break with the earlier ones. On the contrary, they partly assume them even while they reveal their inadequacy—just at the crucial points, indeed, where we might expect the immature and incautious Stephen to be inadequate. Consequently, although the theory in *Ulysses* is more adequate, it does not in itself form a completely satisfactory aesthetic either. Its greater strength lies rather in its correction of the earlier unbalance, its firmer grasp of the subtle, complex relations of art, artist and society—an insight that, theoretical though it is, nevertheless marks a significant shift from one book to the other.

There are three major, interrelated problems that Stephen fails to solve in his theory in the *Portrait*, problems that arise from and reflect his wider attitudes: the relation between aesthetic value and moral value; the difference between aesthetic beauty and natural beauty; and the relation between aesthetic form and aesthetic meaning. In each case, to follow out his ideas is to find ourselves reach the impasse of his immaturity.

I

Stephen, like Joyce himself, begins his theory not with art, but with beauty in general, and he makes the same assumptions and uses the same terminology about it as did his creator. In the first place, both assume that beauty lies not in the eye of the beholder but rather in the object beheld—it is an objective quality, though one that satisfies (as they argue) a special desire to behold it. This desire they call the "esthetic appetite"; the actual beholding "esthetic apprehension"; and they spend most of their time analysing what this latter consists in, for they both also assume that the phases or stages of the beholding correspond to the different characteristics in the object that together constitute its beauty.

Before they turn to this, however, they have to distinguish the "esthetic appetite" from the various appetites that direct other human activities. Every action is directed by an "appetite" seeking to possess

its particular end or "good", but the "esthetic appetite" can be distinguished from others very simply: its end, beauty, cannot be phys-
ically possessed. Like truth, it can only be "spiritually" possessed.
What distinguishes beauty from truth is that the "intellectual appetite"
seeks "the most satisfying relations of the *intelligible*", while the
aesthetic appetite seeks "the most satisfying relations of the *sensible*",
What distinguishes both appetites, however, is that all others are
purely *physical*—mere "desire or loathing", the almost involuntary
reaction of the flesh towards or away from anything. These physical
appetites (or reactions) they call *kinetic*. Beauty, on the other hand,
raises the mind above desire and loathing, arousing only a spiritual
contemplation: "Beauty . . . awakens, or ought to awaken, or induces,
or ought to induce, an esthetic stasis . . . called forth, prolonged
and at last dissolved by what I call the rhythm of beauty" [206].

The most interesting thing about this distinction of appetites is the
way Stephen applies it. He quotes a casual sentence from Aquinas on
which he erects the elaborate structures of his argument: *Pulchra sunt
quae visa placent*: that is beautiful the apprehension of which pleases.
The word "visa", he says, can cover aesthetic apprehensions of all
kinds, but vague as it is, it is nevertheless "clear enough to keep away
good and evil which excite desire and loathing" [207–208]. In other
words, the distinction between the spiritual and the kinetic appetites
is used primarily to keep aesthetics and morals distinct: kinetic ends,
he argues, are quite improper in the spiritual realm of beauty and
art. The conclusion to be drawn from all this is simple but fundamental: didacticism, which is directly moral, and pornography, which
is directly immoral, are equally invalid categories in aesthetics.
Stephen, like the young Joyce, sweeps away both the praise and the
criticism of the pious as equally irrelevant to the true business of art
and of the artist. But we might well notice that the distinction here
is extremely sharp—so sharp, indeed, that Stephen (like many other
similar theorists) falls straight into the trap such distinctions may
conceal. He manages at one stroke to cut art off from *all* "physical"
responses—and by implication from *any* moral activity of the whole
man. When the maturer Stephen talks about *kinesis* in *Ulysses*, this
assumption is abandoned and the term takes on a rather different, and
more satisfactory, meaning. In the *Portrait*, however, he is caught in a
fallacy he does not perceive, in a way that (as we shall see) Joyce
himself was not. Stephen makes no distinction between moral values
and the values of morality, presumably because he cannot see any; he
is, as we realize, too much in revolt against his society, too much
concerned with his individual destiny. The result is hardly surprising:
already, at the very outset of his theory, in trying to explain the activity for the sake of which he must reject his society, he fails to see
that art is far more complex than his theory, and more complex be-

cause it necessarily engages human sympathies, rejections, feelings, thoughts and judgments, even as it gives them another value in ordering them.

We might illustrate the general point Stephen is concerned to make and also its limitations with two passages from *Ulysses*, for the point has an important bearing not only on *Joyce's* attitudes but also on how we read that book itself. When, for example, Mr. Bloom dips into a work entitled *Sweets of Sin*, his response is portrayed as completely kinetic; it is a simple reaction to the kinetic prose he is reading:

> Warmth showered gently over him, cowing his flesh. Flesh yielded amid rumpled clothes. Whites of eyes swooning up. His nostrils arched themselves for prey. Melting breast ointments *(for him! For Raoul!)* Armpits' oniony sweat. Fishgluey slime *(her heaving embonpoint!)*. Feel! Press! Crushed! Sulphur dung of lions! [*U*, 233/236]

On the other hand, when he listens later on to Simon Dedalus singing, the "mercy of beauty" achieves a very different result [*U*, 269-271/273-276]. The song induces in Bloom what seems to be an aesthetic *stasis*, prolonged and at last dissolved by the sheer beauty of the song:

> —*Come!*
> It soared, a bird, it held its flight, a swift pure cry, soar silver orb it leaped serene, speeding, sustained, to come, don't spin it out too long long breath he breath long life, soaring high, high resplendent, aflame, crowned, high in the effulgence symbolistic, high, of the ethereal bosom, high, of the high vast irradiation everywhere all soaring all around about the all, the endlessnessnessness . . .
> —*To me!*
> Siopold!
> Consumed. [*U*, 271/275-276]

This is the kind of result Stephen evidently has in mind when he speaks of "the luminous silent stasis of esthetic pleasure, a spiritual state very like to that cardiac condition which the Italian physiologist Luigi Galvani, using a phrase almost as beautiful as Shelley's, called the enchantment of the heart" [213]. Yet to suppose that *no* kinetic appetites were involved in a *stasis* like this is to miss the important fact that to Bloom the song has a deeply felt significance, and that its beauty to him derives from the way it arouses and orders his feelings and memories and lusts and judgments. It is the love-song from *Martha*, and so it quickens both his complex feelings about his pitiful flirtation with Martha Clifford and his memories about the first time he saw Molly, his wife, whose present infidelity is very much in his mind. His sense of frustration and of loneliness, his judgment of the singer—all these are carefully, and properly, interwoven by Joyce into the fabric of Bloom's experience of the song. It has a meaning and value that can only be called moral just because it effects a *stasis* that is wider than Stephen's "spiritual" suggests. And the relevance of this truth becomes increasingly important as we go on with his theory in the *Portrait*, for it is something he nowhere properly recognizes.

II

The second problem—the difference between aesthetic and natural beauty—is very largely a development and a heightening of the first.

Having distinguished the "spiritual" appetites and ends from the "kinetic" ones, and having also distinguished truth from beauty, Stephen can now turn to the central act of "esthetic apprehension" itself. Here, both Stephen and the young Joyce follow (but only roughly) the Scholastics' three-fold analysis of any act of ordinary apprehension. Firstly, there is the stage where we perceive the physical presence and unity of an object—what Stephen calls its "wholeness" or *integritas*. Secondly—and of course these stages are more logical than chronological—our minds engage in analysis, perceiving the object in its conceptual or intelligible aspect: the process in which we reach an intellectual "recognition" of the object, seeing it as something shaped and informed by a "universal". This aspect is presumably what Stephen calls the object's *consonantia* or "harmony", but the way he describes it marks his first significant departure from the Scholastic analysis—one to which we shall have to return in a moment. But he also parts company with the Scholastics about the third stage as well, and, even more important, with both the formulations of the young Joyce himself (as we find them in the notebooks) and the formulations offered in *Stephen Hero*. To the Scholastic, the third stage of apprehension is the mind's expressing its perception of the object in a *concept* and ultimately in a *word*. But although this view is implied later on in *Ulysses*, it is not what Stephen thinks in the *Portrait* nor is it what the young Joyce himself thought. The differences are subtle and not immediately obvious; nevertheless, they are so significant of wider issues and wider attitudes that they have to be made clear from the outset.

We may start with Joyce's own remarks about "esthetic apprehension" in his notebooks. When he himself reached this third stage of his analysis, he recognized that he had to agree with the Scholastics that *any* object, if it could be perceived in the twofold way described so far, could also be called "beautiful"—but only in their general, transcendental sense of Beauty, the sense in which it can be regarded as a property of all Creation, like Truth or Unity. But of course this metaphysical or religious sense of Beauty is not what we mean by *aesthetic* beauty, which is not a property of all objects nor always necessarily perceived in those that do possess it. So, in his notebooks (Gorman, pp. 134–5), Joyce goes on to meet this problem by arguing that aesthetic beauty is perceived only in a special third stage of apprehension, a stage that is *specifically* aesthetic. He speaks of it as an "activity of satisfaction", and claims that in practice the words "beautiful" and "ugly" are "applied chiefly to the third activity, with regard, that is, to the nature, degree and duration of the satisfaction resultant from the apprehension of any sensible object." This is probably his first formal attempt to define what he himself was seeking in art, but clearly it could hardly do as it stands. For one thing, it is too vague really to explain anything about beauty; and for another, it puts the emphasis where Joyce was anxious not to put it—on a subjective response rather than the properties of the object itself.

Logically, therefore, the next formulation is that in *Stephen Hero* [213], which attempts to get over this difficulty by introducing what is perhaps the best-known of all Joyce's terms: "epiphany". In a sense, this concept is central to all his subsequent thinking about art and its relations with life, his understanding of his own activity as an artist and his whole conception of its meaning and value. But although his art embodies his developing understanding of the term, and although the art of the *Portrait* implies a fully mature grasp of what it involves, it is not until *Ulysses* that he can show *Stephen* reaching even a proper theoretical grasp of it. In *Stephen Hero*, therefore, we find a far cruder conception of "epiphany" than in *Ulysses*, yet one that does, at least temporarily, get round the immediate problem Joyce found himself confronted with by his argument in the notebooks. By "epiphany", Stephen explains, he means a "sudden spiritual manifestation"; and he uses the term to explain what happens in the third stage of aesthetic apprehension:

> After the analysis which discovers the second quality the mind makes the only logically possible synthesis and discovers the third quality. This is the moment which I call epiphany. First we recognize that the object is *one* integral thing, then we recognize that it is an organized composite structure, a *thing* in fact: finally, when the relation of the parts is exquisite, when the parts are adjusted to the special point, we recognize that it is *that* thing which it is. Its soul, its whatness, leaps to us from the vestment of its appearance. The soul of the commonest object, the structure of which is so adjusted, seems to us radiant. The object achieves its epiphany.

What this tries to do is obvious enough: firstly, to show how something in the object, its true inner nature, corresponds to a stage of its perception by a subject; and secondly, to show how this third stage follows from the other two. Having apprehended the physical presence of the object, its *integritas*, and the conceptual structure of the object, its *consonantia*, we now apprehend it as matter everywhere interpenetrated with intelligible structure, as the composition of matter and form that makes it the thing it is, so that it appears luminous, producing what Stephen calls *claritas*. Stephen also equates this with the Scholastic *quidditas* of an object, but the Scholastic term really applies to the universal form. What Stephen means is something like *haecceitas*, the individual this-ness of an object; he is closer to Hopkins, with his "inscape", than to Aquinas. Unfortunately, he never clarifies the relation of the objective and the subjective aspects of the epiphany —the relation between the *self-revelation* of the object itself and the meaning that the beholder *gives* to it in beholding it. That question has to be left until *Ulysses* when it moves to the centre of the stage, for it is there seen to be a crucial one for the artist and the ordinary man alike: it involves the whole problem of the *values* we perceive in, or give to, our experience. At this stage, however, it is enough for Stephen to have worked out what it is we mean when we speak of the "beauty" of an object, and to have freed the artist—whose business is with beauty—from the encumbrance of both moralistic and merely conventional notions of beauty.

To turn from the notebooks and *Stephen Hero* to the *Portrait*, however, is to perceive a startling difference of emphasis—a difference in the way Stephen conceives *consonantia*, and closely connected with that, in the way he conceives *claritas*. In each case, the difference— subtle as it may seem—is of paramount importance, and in each case again it is a matter not of what he changes, but rather of what he leaves out: which is to say, what considerations he ignores, what factors limit his whole outlook.

At a first glance, the differences seem hardly to matter. With *consonantia*, for example, he seems only to restate what is said in *Stephen Hero*:

Stephen Hero:

Analysis then. The mind considers the object in whole and in part, *in relation to itself and to other objects,* examines the balance of its parts, contemplates the form of the object, traverses every cranny of the structure. ([*SH*, 212]; my italics)

Portrait:

you pass from point to point, led by its formal lines; you apprehend it as balanced part against part within its limits; you feel the rhythm of its structure. In other words, the synthesis of immediate perception is followed by the analysis of apprehension. Having first felt that it is *one* thing you feel now that it is a *thing*. You apprehend it as complex, multiple, divisible, separable, made up of its parts, the result of its parts and their sum, harmonious. That is *consonantia*. [212]

The crucial difference lies in the dropping of the phrase I have italicized in the former—or rather, in the dropping of any reference to *the world outside the object itself.* With *claritas* the difference is rather more obvious: it consists in the dropping of the whole notion of "epiphany"—and with it, once again, any reference to the spiritual insight, *the imaginative-moral activity,* of the beholder:

> When you have apprehended [the object] . . . as one thing and have then analysed it according to its form and apprehended it as a thing you make the only synthesis which is logically and esthetically permissible. You see that it is that thing which it is and no other thing. The radiance of which he [Aquinas] speaks is the scholastic *quidditas,* the *whatness* of a thing. [213]

Why these emphases in the *Portrait* do not seem to matter at a first glance is simply that at this point Stephen is talking about beauty in general, beauty as it may be found in *any* object. And if we think of the beauty of trees or oranges, for example, it is reasonable enough to limit our analysis to the qualities of the object itself. Whether we find it acceptable or not as an account of beauty, it provokes no immediate, fundamental objections as applied to natural objects. Applied to art, however, it most certainly does—and this is just where Stephen wants to apply it.

Art, says Stephen (and he is echoing Joyce's own definition), is "the human disposition of sensible or intelligible matter for an esthetic end" [207]. What he means by an "esthetic end" is clearly the satisfaction of the three stages of "esthetic apprehension": the work of art must possess *integritas, consonantia* and *claritas.* Yet if we now apply Stephen's account of these terms to art, we can see how narrow his conception of it is. *Consonantia* amounts only to a purely formal relationship of parts; "structure" could be no more than pattern, any pattern; there is no real awareness of what the "harmony" of art is a harmony *of.* Even the phrase about "the disposition of sensible or intelligible matter" evades the problem, for since Stephen regards *all* objects of beauty as composed of sensible and intelligible matter, it hardly distinguishes the "matter" of art in any way. The truth is that Stephen's theory nowhere does; with the result that he does not, and cannot, suggest how one "harmony" can be deeper, more significant, than another. His definitions admit no possibility of perceiving a qualitative difference in the *consonantia* of (say) Poe's "The Bells" and Blake's "London." It is impossible to think that *Joyce* believed this, and the phrase in *Stephen Hero* about the mind considering the object "in relation to itself and to other objects" does at least make an attempt to meet the problem. But for Stephen in the *Portrait, consonantia* seems only a matter of mere organization rather than one of imaginative coherence. Once again, he cuts art off from the life which goes into it and from which its "harmony" derives significance.

So, too, with *claritas.* The "whatness" of a poem, for example, is rather different from the "whatness" of a natural object. One thing they have in common may be, as *Stephen Hero* suggests, that to perceive either a spiritual activity on the part of the beholder is necessary, and certainly this is true of the poem, even if a good deal more has to be said about what the activity consists in and how it engages with the work. But to leave this activity of aesthetic apprehension out altogether, as Stephen does in the *Portrait*, is in effect to ignore what makes a *human* disposition of sensible or intelligible matter different from a natural disposition of sensible or intelligible matter: that is, the human (or, broadly, the moral) significance of art, its capacity to speak the language of human life in a way that natural objects do not.

Yet if we look at the *Portrait* as a whole, it is hardly very surprising that Stephen should fall into this confusion between nature and art. When he thinks of his own artistic ambitions, he can never clearly distinguish between what he feels is a natural and irresistible force in his life, his individual character and talent, and his own free choices as a moral agent. He feels himself impelled by his own nature to do what he must—rejecting the lesser claims of society, home and religion —and he feels it so strongly that he cannot conceive his inescapable moral responsibilities as a man very clearly. Thus art appears to him largely as the exercise of a natural talent, the product of a natural power in the individual (albeit a force disciplined by a conscious sense of formal craftsmanship); as yet he cannot see that it involves the matured feelings, values and choices of the artist as a man, and a far profounder discipline. His own callow poetry in the novel ("Are you not weary of ardent ways" and so on) is, as we perceive, an illustration of, and a critical judgment on, not only the theory but also on the underlying attitudes the theory expresses.

III

Thus the third problem raised by the theory—the relation between aesthetic form and aesthetic meaning—inevitably emerges from the other two, and Stephen's failure to solve this one is already implicit in his failure to solve them. Yet it does also have a special importance in that it raises most acutely the difficulty of interpreting *Joyce's* attitude to art, and it is perhaps worth examining with particular care in order to avoid confusions about that. For this whole problem of aesthetic form and aesthetic meaning would never arise—or alternatively it could be regarded as solved—if only we could attribute to Stephen, and by implication to Joyce, some convenient set of metaphysical beliefs—like those of Aquinas, for example. This in fact is precisely what many of Joyce's critics have done. And yet if we look at what the relevant works actually say, we shall find that to do so is to miss the real point of Stephen's theorizing in both the *Portrait* and *Ulysses*.

We may begin with the question that has obviously been becoming increasingly urgent as we proceed with the theory: where in his argument does Stephen discuss—or even account for—the *meaningfulness* of art, those subtle relations with life that others have tried to explain with terms like "imitation", "universality", "revelation", "express", "symbol", and so on? Certainly the answer does not lie in his definition of art itself: as we have seen, the "esthetic end" involves no distinction between art and other kinds of beautiful things, nor does the term "sensible or intelligible matter". At a first glance, perhaps, this latter phrase may seem to include the possibility of *truth* as well as beauty in art (since truth is "the most satisfying relations of the intelligible"), but once we look at it more closely, we firstly begin to wonder whether the alternative of sensible *or* intelligible is really accurate, for if anything is "sensible" it is surely also "intelligible" in that it must embody a conceptual form that enables us to recognize what it is; and then we realize that, just because the phrase is so loose, it cannot help to distinguish a work of art from a chair (say) or even a tree. All are "sensible or intelligible matter"; all may serve an "esthetic end" in that all may be "esthetically apprehended"; and logic-chopping about the rest of the definition—about "human disposition . . . for an esthetic end"—may be relevant to the attitudes proper to artists, but it tells us nothing about *art* except that it is made by human beings. The kind of "truth" Stephen's definition includes in art, therefore, could only be (if anything) the transcendental "truth" that all objects have been said to possess because their "forms" or "essences" bring our minds into conformity with God's Intelligence (since all "forms" are His creation and also the metaphysical aspect of things that makes them "intelligible" to us). But like transcendental Beauty, this is not the kind of quality we mean if we speak of the "truth" of a work of art: that is a truth to human experience, a poetic truth, and one, moreover, that is capable of *qualitative* judgments. If, therefore (as some readers suppose), Stephen *is* trying to reconcile truth and beauty in art, his definition makes only the vaguest and most ineffectual gesture towards doing so.

Nor does he do very much better with his manipulation of the term *stasis*. It emerges in the course of his exposition that *stasis*, as well as being the product of beauty, is also "the tragic emotion", a balanced combination of pity and terror. And of course pity and terror are responses to life:

> Pity is the feeling which arrests the mind in the presence of whatsoever is grave and constant in human sufferings and unites it with the human sufferer. Terror is the feeling which arrests the mind in the presence

of whatsoever is grave and constant in human sufferings and unites it with the secret cause. [204]

On this basis, only a genuinely serious art will produce *stasis*, and it is a seriousness that is capable of being judged as more or less profound: here, it would seem, is the relationship between art and life we are seeking. And significantly enough, the young Joyce himself used much these terms in his notebooks when he tried to define comedy as well as tragedy: the aim of comedy, he argues, is to produce the feeling of "joy"; this joy derives from the contemplation of "whatever is substantial or accidental in human fortunes"; and comedy is to be judged by whether the joy is excited by the more or the less "substantial" (Gorman, pp. 96–7).

Yet, as Joyce himself must have recognized, the problem is still there: the seriousness of art does not really depend on its *subject-matter*. Even Stephen himself seems dimly aware of this in the *Portrait*, and he tries to solve it by simply identifying the *stasis* that *all* beauty ought to produce with the *stasis* that serious subject-matter ought to produce:

> Beauty . . . awakens, or ought to awaken, or induces, or ought to induce, an esthetic stasis, *an ideal pity or an ideal terror,* a stasis called forth, prolonged and at last dissolved by what I call the rhythm of beauty. [206]

Unfortunately, this simple identification of the two kinds of *stasis* solves nothing, for it leads Stephen straight into the same kind of fallacy as he fell into with *consonantia* and *claritas*: this "ideal pity" and "ideal terror" may apply to the beauty of art, but they do not apply to the beauty of natural objects. We may perhaps speak in his fashion about some picture of an orange, for example, but we should hardly do so about an orange. Not that the difficulty with the theory has anything to do with representational art—that, except as a test case, is really beside the point. It is rather that Stephen explains nothing about the significance that art possesses *as* art, and how it is that we can in fact judge it; he scarcely recognizes that poetic meaning and imaginative truth are created in art, let alone offer any discussion of what these qualities are.

Once again the difference between the *Portrait* and Joyce's other early writings underlines how much of his own thinking Joyce deliberately refrained from here attributing to Stephen. The paper on "Drama and Life" that Joyce delivered at college, for instance, contains at least one passage that the Stephen of the *Portrait* could not have spoken. Art, Joyce maintained, became false to itself once it submitted to the demands of religion or morality or romantic idealism; it was equally falsified by submitting to the demands of the Aesthete, the critic who is concerned only with Beauty: "Beauty is the swerga of the aesthete; but truth has a more ascertainable and more real dominion. Art is true to itself when it deals with truth" [*CW*, 43–44]. This is to put the matter crudely, of course, but at least it does suggest an insight much wider than Stephen's in the *Portrait*, and it does point directly to the major assumption of the theory outlined in *Stephen Hero*. In this work, the passage where Stephen expounds his theories to Cranly, which forms the basis for the passage in the *Portrait* where he expounds them to Lynch, is overshadowed by the longer and more striking argument of the paper he delivers at college —the argument for which Joyce drew on his own papers. Nothing of this argument remains in the *Portrait* and very little of the Stephen it represents; on the other hand, the same line of thought (though in different terms) does reappear in *Ulysses*. The reason is not hard to see: for all the traces of Aquinas in it, Stephen's paper owes far more to Shelley's *Defence of Poetry*, and it represents a Stephen, and a Joyce, who are Romantics no doubt, but Romantics really trying to meet their central problem—the relation of art and life—and reaching for a solution that will transcend the limitations of Romanticism without rejecting its genuine insights. The solution is only adumbrated here; like the concept of "epiphany", it was to take on a deeper meaning with greater experience. But already, as even a quick glance at the argument shows, Joyce had grasped what was far beyond a character like the Stephen of the *Portrait*: the need for "the classical temper".

The central theme of the argument is the same as Shelley's: art as the discovery and re-creation of values. Only the poet, Shelley had argued, can penetrate the outward circumstances of his society to the eternal truths about man and his universe, which it is the task of the mere "reasoners and mechanists" to apply to the current needs of the time. The fictions of Homer (to take a relevant example) are not mere representations of barbaric society now long outdated. Under the local customs and beliefs of the age, under the dress of a heroic society, are revelations of permanent value because of permanent validity. "Homer embodied the ideal perfection of his age in human character", inspiring his audience to become as like his heroes as they could by identification with figures that expressed "the truth and beauty of friendship, patriotism, and persevering devotion to an object". It makes no difference that the heroes are not quite perfect:

> a poet considers the vices of his contemporaries as a temporary dress in which his creations must be arrayed, and which cover without concealing the eternal proportions of their beauty.

Indeed, the eternal truth and beauty the poet reveals are so dazzling that it is probably necessary for him to "temper this planetary music for mortal ears" by dressing his characters in the costume and customs of the time. The poet, then, has a double task—to represent the world around him, and to reveal through it the "unchangeable forms of human nature". Merely to catalogue the facts of the world about him is to write a "story" not a "poem".[2]

As soon as Stephen starts talking in his paper about the poet as the "mediator between the world of his experience and the world of his dreams" [*SH*, 77], we recognize the characteristic Shelleyan flavour. It is absurd, says Stephen, for "a criticism itself established upon homilies to prohibit the elective courses of the artist in his *revelation* of the beautiful"—the emphasis is Stephen's. We are told that "every age must look for its sanction to its poets and philosophers"; that the poet is the "intense centre of the life of his age"; that "he alone is capable of absorbing in himself the life that surrounds him and of flinging it abroad again amid planetary music"; that critics must set their calculations by the "poetic phenomenon"—

> It is time for them to acknowledge that here the imagination has contemplated intensely the truth of the being of the visible world and that beauty, the splendour of truth, has been born. The age, though it bury itself fathoms deep in formulas and machinery, has need of these realities which alone give and sustain life and it must await from those chosen centres of vivification the force to live, the security for life which can come to it only from them. Thus the spirit of man makes a continual affirmation. [*SH*, 80]

Thus he also distinguishes between mere "literature" and "poetry", the one concerned with the "manners and customs of societies", the externals, and the other with the essential and "unalterable laws" of society.

The artist has "twin faculties, a selective faculty and a reproductive faculty". He has to "disentangle the subtle soul of the image from its mesh of defining circumstances"—to catch what he elsewhere calls an "epiphany"—and to "re-embody" it in the most suitable artistic circumstances. This language is far from exact, of course, and the difficulties it raises are never discussed, but it is sufficient for Stephen's next major point—an attack on the "romantic temper". This is the artistic attitude that finds "no fit abode here for its ideals and chooses therefore to behold them under insensible figures"; the attitude, presumably, that damages a good deal of Shelley's own work and some of the French Symbolists', by producing remote, unsubstantial images whose feet never quite touch the ground. The dangers of the romantic temper, says Stephen, are to be remedied by the adoption of the "classical style". The classical temper, in opposition to the romantic, "chooses rather to bend upon these present things and so to work upon them and fashion them that the quick intelligence may go beyond them to their meaning which is still unuttered".

[2] *Shelley's Literary and Philosophical Criticism,* ed. John Shawcross, London, 1909, esp. pp. 128–30.

In other words, Stephen like the young Joyce himself is advocating art that combines an intense concern with values, so that it becomes an imaginative "criticism of life", with a technique firmly based upon a realistic fidelity to ordinary experience. "Life", as Joyce said in "Drama and Life", "we must accept as we see it before our eyes, men and women as we meet them in the real world, not as we apprehend them in the world of faery" [*CW*, 45]. It is hardly surprising therefore that Joyce the Romantic rebel felt more at home with the art of Ibsen than with that of his Irish contemporaries at the turn of the century or with the kind of poetry that Stephen in the *Portrait* composes. The artist had to recognize the wider meaning and implications of his art; his devotion to it had to be in the interests of "spiritual truth" and "affirmation". A mere aesthete, as he said in *The Day of the Rabblement*, "has a floating will" (Gorman, p. 72). Ibsen combined the artist's "lofty impersonal power" with an admirably "classical" technique. In contrast, George Russell, as reported in *Ulysses*, advocates "formless spiritual essences" as the proper substance of art. Stephen's unspoken response to him there—"Hold to the now, the here, through which all future plunges to the past"—is in part a demand for the discipline of a technique committed to everyday life. But since Stephen has by that stage reached a rather maturer awareness of the same problems the young Joyce also had to face, it is also something more.

Returning to the *Portrait* with all this in mind, we find one of Stephen's remarks there particularly revealing. Speaking of his theory of beauty, he adds:

> So far as this side of esthetic philosophy extends, Aquinas will carry me all along the line. When we come to the phenomena of artistic conception, artistic gestation and artistic reproduction I require a new terminology and a new personal experience. [209]

On the other hand, he obviously does not see the difficulties into which his "pennyworths of wisdom" from St Thomas have led him. Nor does he see how much more acute those difficulties are made by his adopting casual ideas from St Thomas without adopting the metaphysics that give the ideas coherence. Thus the problem of the poetic meaning and truth of art is capable of *some* kind of solution if we hold a philosophy that gives "intelligibility" a metaphysical range: if we believe, that is, that the intelligibility of art ought to reveal and reflect the intelligibility inherent in all things in the world. A Thomist aesthetic could be developed in this way (as Maritain, for one, shows[3]); and Hermeticism or Neo-Platonism or some kinds of

[3] See J. Maritain, *Art and Scholasticism*, trans. J. F. Scanlan, London, 1930, pp. 24 ff., 162 ff. But see J. Mitchell Morse, *The Sympathetic Alien*, p. 94, on the difficulties of making Aquinas yield a theory of artistic *creation*.

Symbolism or Transcendentalism encourage the same approach too. But unless we foist a philosophy of this kind upon Stephen, or upon Joyce, the theory in the *Portrait* remains cripplingly limited.

The fact is, however, that neither Joyce nor Stephen accepts any such metaphysical philosophy. If there are vestigial traces of Shelleyan Platonism in the paper in *Stephen Hero* they are clearly out of place beside the arguments for "the classical temper", and in *Ulysses*, we find, the whole argument is reformulated precisely in order to avoid the slightest suggestion that art reflects some other metaphysical world. And even in the *Portrait* Stephen's attitude is perfectly clear and definite. He dismisses some possible interpretations of what Aquinas meant by *claritas* and (although he is probably wrong about Aquinas) his reasons for doing so are of the highest importance:

> It would lead you to believe that he had in mind symbolism or idealism, the supreme quality of beauty being a light from some other world, the idea of which the matter is but the shadow, the reality of which it is but the symbol. I thought he might mean that *claritas* is the artistic discovery and representation of the divine purpose in anything or a force of generalization which would make the esthetic image a universal one, make it outshine its proper conditions. [213]

He rejects all these interpretations, and since he consistently stands by his rejection, since it is also the attitude of *Stephen Hero*, and since it is even elaborated still further in *Ulysses*, we must take it, I believe, as Joyce's rejection too. We could say, indeed, that it is a premise of the whole art of *Ulysses* itself, a corollary (though as put here, only a negative one) of "the classical temper". Joyce never believed that art represents ideas that can be extraneously formulated, or some supernatural "Reality". He is obviously at one with Stephen at least in trying to prevent art from disappearing altogether into any ethical or social or scientific or metaphysical Truth it is supposed to serve.

But if we can appreciate the force both of Stephen's rejection in the *Portrait* and of his contempt for the enormous pretensions, the "literary talk", of some of the Symbolist theories of the time, we have to admit that the mere rejection, however just it may be, is not enough. The basic problem still remains. Correct up to a point, but with a still limited insight into the issues he raises, he seems to suggest that if a work of art had *any* kind of universal meaning it would "outshine its proper conditions". The old term "universality" may be inadequate, but to put nothing in its place is again to cut art off from life altogether.

Of course, we could do what many of Joyce's critics do, and save Stephen's theory by interpreting it in the light of—or rather, by conflating it with—ideas from outside the *Portrait*. Some want to add the notion of "epiphany" from *Stephen Hero* to give a moral content to *claritas*; some want to add emotions, attitudes, values, to give content to *consonantia* and *stasis*; some want to add Aristotelian or Thomist metaphysics to give meaning to "intelligibility". But whether these are acceptable as Joyce's views or not (and I hope that even so brief an examination of his writings will have suggested which are and which are not), all these interpretations import ideas *into* the *Portrait*, all add to what Joyce makes Stephen actually say. What is even more important, however, all such additions finally result in obscuring the crucial *dramatic* logic of the theory in both the *Portrait* and in *Ulysses* as well. For Joyce clearly limits Stephen's understanding of art just as he limits his understanding of life; what Stephen does not see about the one is what he does not know of the other. And his explicit rejection of any metaphysical view of art is significant just because it does lead him to an impasse, to a central problem he has to face as soon as he realizes what it is, just as Joyce himself had to face it: how does art have moral significance and of what kind? how, indeed, do *any* of our activities have moral significance, and of what kind? These are necessarily the questions he confronts in *Ulysses*.

To iron out the difficulties of his theory in the *Portrait,* therefore, is to miss the most important function it serves: its limitations focus exactly the limitations of Stephen's still "uncreated soul". At best, he can achieve an uneasy combination of "beauty" and "truth" as distinct and unrelated essentials, but it is precisely the lack of relation that robs them of significance and handicaps the theory as a whole. By ignoring the contexts of human experience in which art is created and apprehended, and the function of the language in which that experience is embodied, Stephen ignores the whole symbolic aspect of art. The result is, in a very pure sense, what has been called the "ontological fallacy"—the belief that "a work of art fulfils its purpose and achieves its value simply by *being*, so that the critic becomes concerned only to demonstrate the mode of its being by descriptive analysis".[4] To ignore the meanings created in a work of art—and particularly to ignore the manner of their presence—is to come perilously close to pure Aestheticism, and this Stephen in effect does. Subtly but inevitably, he suggests that as the artist is isolated from his society so art is isolated from life. His rejection of *kinesis* seems all too like a rejection of emotion rather than a demand for its purification, for a true impersonality; it hints at a fear of reality rather than a welcoming acceptance of it in order to transform it and express it in another mode. In the long run, Stephen extends the exile of the artist to the exile of art.

In short, both he and his theory lack real engagement with life. For all his desire and intention:

[4] David Daiches, *Literary Essays,* Edinburgh and London, 1956, p. 173.

Yes! Yes! Yes! He would create proudly out of the freedom and power
of his soul . . . a living thing [170]

he has not yet achieved the necessary moral maturity, the necessary
kind of power and freedom. His attitude towards his present circumstances of life is little more than a simple repudiation, a sharp,
almost involuntary, reaction; in a word, a sort of personal *kinesis*. He
uses the word "life", but only as an empty counter. He lacks the
proper freedom that consists in mature understanding, a willingness
to accept life as it is given as the necessary medium of one's own
labour, even while one criticizes it at the same time. His alienation
from his society and its values, though by no means irresponsible or
unjustified, is not yet self-critical, impersonal detachment. What has
to be left until *Ulysses* is a richer context of experience; the missing
theory of artistic expression, which can explain how subject and object,
meaning and quiddity, feeling and fact, are *fused* by the artist in his
very medium, language; the recognition of how art, and the artist,
achieve appropriate freedom and life; the healing of the split between
"beauty" and "truth". There, the insights represented by the embryonic
concept of "epiphanies", the callow essays on "Drama and Life",
"James Clarence Mangan" and "Art and Life", and by other aspects
of Joyce's own jottings in his notebooks, are developed, re-formulated
and now redress the balance. In short, Stephen's aesthetic is made to
grow and change as Stephen himself is made to grow and change.

It would seem, then, that although Stephen and the young Joyce
shared a common desire to emphasize that quality of art Kant called
"purposiveness without purpose", and to dissociate the ("static") appetites satisfied by beauty and art from the ("kinetic") ones of ordinary
life, Joyce himself did not fall into the same traps as Stephen: of
supposing that human experience could really be divided in this way,
or that, if the purposes of art are not in any crude sense moral, it therefore has no moral significance and its meaning is therefore negligible.
The mature artist obviously saw through his immature hero's theories
well enough, and obviously arranged the elements of his own thinking
to achieve the maximum dramatic effect. The importance of the theory
in the *Portrait*—and in *Ulysses* too, for that matter—is not as a standard by which to appreciate or to judge Joyce's art. Rather, it is as a
focus for the problems, which are fundamentally moral problems, with
which both works are concerned as dramatic novels.

The Problem of Distance
in *A Portrait of the Artist*

by Wayne C. Booth

[NOTE: *In the portion of* The Rhetoric of Fiction *which precedes this selection, Booth discusses the difficulties in interpretation caused by the use of irony in works of past centuries. He finds three causes of such difficulties: lack of adequate warning that irony is at work; excessive complexity, subtlety, or privacy of the norms to be inferred; and vivid psychological realism, which works against our capacity for judgment. The presence or absence of such difficulties does not necessarily say anything about the quality of a work. But it can make a great difference in how hard the reader must work to see the story in its own true light.*]

Everyone recognizes that each of these three sources of difficulty is present in some modern fiction, frequently in forms much more deceptive than anything encountered in earlier work. Any one of them alone can give trouble. And in some modern fiction all three are present. There is no warning, either explicitly or in the form of gross disparity of word and deed; the relationship of the ironic narrator to the author's norms is an extremely complex one, and the norms are themselves subtle and private; and the narrator's own mental vitality dominates the scene and wins our sympathy.

It is in the last of these three that modern fiction has gone far beyond anything experienced before Flaubert. Jane Austen's implicit apology for Emma said, in effect, "Emma's vision is your vision; therefore forgive her." But modern authors have learned how to provide this apology in much more insistent form. The deep plunges of modern inside views, the various streams-of-consciousness that attempt to give the reader an effect of living thought and sensation, are capable of blinding us to the possibility of our making judgments not shared by the narrator or reflector himself.

If a master puzzle maker had set out to give us the greatest pos-

sible difficulty, he could not have done more than has been done in
some modern works in which this effect of deep involvement is
combined with the implicit demand that we maintain our capacity
for ironic judgment. The trouble with *Moll Flanders,* such a genius
of confusion might be imagined as saying to himself, is that the
obvious differences between the female heroine and the author provide too many clues. Let us then write a book that will look like the
author's autobiography, using many details from his own life and
opinions. But we cannot be satisfied with moral problems, which are
after all much less subject to dispute than intellectual and aesthetic
matters. Let us then call for the reader's precise judgment on a very
elaborate set of opinions and actions in which the hero is sometimes
right, sometimes slightly wrong, and sometimes absurdly astray. Just
to make sure that things are not too obvious, let us finally bind the
reader so tightly to the consciousness of the ambiguously misguided
protagonist that nothing will interfere with his delight in inferring
the precise though varying degrees of distance that operate from
point to point throughout the book. We can be sure that some readers
will take the book as strictly autobiographical; others will go sadly
astray in overlooking ironies that are intended and in discovering
ironies that are not there. But for the rare reader who can make his
way through this jungle, the delight will be great indeed.

The giant whom we all must wrestle with in this regard is clearly
Joyce. Except for occasional outbursts of bravado nobody has ever
really claimed that Joyce is clear. In all the skeleton keys and class-
room guides there is an open assumption that his later works, *Ulysses* and *Finnegans Wake,* cannot be read; they can only be studied.
Joyce himself was always explicating his works, and it is clear that
he saw nothing wrong with the fact that they could not be thought
of as standing entirely on their own feet. The reader's problems are
handled, if they are to be handled at all, by rhetoric provided outside
the work.

But the difficulties with distance that are pertinent here cannot
be removed by simple study. Obscure allusions can be looked up,
patterns of imagery and theme can be traced; gradually over the
years a good deal of lore has accumulated, and about some of it by
now there is even a certain amount of agreement. But about the
more fundamental matters the skeleton keys and guides are of little help, because unfortunately they do not agree, they do not agree
at all. It is fine to know that in *Ulysses* Stephen stands in some way
for Telemachus and Bloom for his wandering father, Ulysses. But
it would also be useful to know whether the work is comic or pathetic or tragic, or, if it is a combination, where the elements fall.
Can two readers be said to have read the same book if one thinks it
ends affirmatively and the other sees the ending as pessimistic? It is

really no explanation to say that Joyce has succeeded in imitating life so well that like life itself his books seem totally ambiguous, totally open to whatever interpretation the reader wants to place on them. Even William Empson, that perceptive and somewhat overly ingenious prophet of ambiguity, finds himself unable to be completely permissive toward conflicting interpretations. In a long, curious essay arguing that the basic movement of *Ulysses* is toward a favorable ending, with the Blooms and Stephen united, he admits that there are difficulties, and that they spring from the kind of book it is: it "not only refuses to tell you the end of the story, it also refuses to tell you what the author thinks would have been a good end to the story." And yet almost in the same breath he can write as if he thought previous critics somehow at fault for not having come to *his* inferences about the book. "By the way, I have no patience with critics who say it is impossible ever to tell whether Joyce means a literary effect to be ironical or not; if they don't know this part isn't funny, they ought to." [1] Well, but why should they be able to? Who is to mediate between Empson and those he attacks, or between Lawrance Thompson, in his interpretation of the book as comedy, and those critics with whom he is "decidedly at odds," Stuart Gilbert, Edmund Wilson, Harry Levin, David Daiches, and T. S. Eliot, each of whom assumes, he says, that "Joyce's artistic mode is essentially a non-comic mode, or that comedy in *Ulysses* is an effect rather than a cause"? [2]

Can it possibly make no difference whether we laugh or do not laugh? Can we defend the book even as a realistic mixture, like life itself, unless we can state with some precision what the ingredients are that have been mixed together?

Rather than pursue such general questions about Joyce's admittedly difficult later works, it will be more useful to look closely at that earlier work for which no skeleton key has been thought necessary, *A Portrait of the Artist as a Young Man* (1916). Everyone seems by now agreed that it is a masterpiece in the modern mode. Perhaps we can accept it as that—indeed accept it as an unquestionably great work from any viewpoint—and still feel free to ask a few irreverent questions.

The structure of this "authorless" work is based on the growth of a sensitive boy to young manhood. The steps in his growth are obviously constructed with great care. Each of the first four sections ends a period of Stephen's life with what Joyce, in an earlier draft, calls an epiphany: a peculiar revelation of the inner reality of an experience, accompanied with great elation, as in a mystical religious experience. Each is followed by the opening of a new chapter on a

---

[1] "The Theme of *Ulysses*," *Kenyon Review*, XVIII (Winter, 1956), 36, 31.
[2] *A Comic Principle in Sterne—Meredith—Joyce* (Oslo, 1954), p. 22.

very prosaic, even depressed level. Now here is clearly a careful structural preparation—for what? For a transformation, or for a merely
cyclical return? Is the final exaltation a release from the depressing
features of Irish life which have tainted the earlier experiences? Or
is it the fifth turn in an endless cycle? And in either case, is Stephen
always to be viewed with the same deadly seriousness with which he
views himself? Is it to artistic maturity that he grows? As the young
man goes into exile from Ireland, goes "to encounter for the millionth
time the reality of experience and to forge in the smithy" of his soul
"the uncreated conscience" of his race, are we to take this, with Harry
Levin, as a fully serious portrait of the artist Dedalus, praying to his
namesake Daedalus, to stand him "now and ever in good stead"? [3]
Or is the inflated style, as Mark Schorer tells us, Joyce's clue that the
young Icarus is flying too close to the sun, with the "excessive lyric
relaxation" of Stephen's final style punctuating "the illusory nature
of the whole ambition"? [4] The young man takes himself and his
flight with deadly solemnity. Should we?

To see the difficulties clearly, let us consider three crucial episodes,
all from the final section: his rejection of the priesthood, his exposition of what he takes to be Thomistic aesthetics, and his composition
of a poem.

Is his rejection of the priesthood a triumph, a tragedy, or merely
a comedy of errors? Most readers, even those who follow the new
trend of reading Stephen ironically, seem to have read it as a triumph:
the artist has rid himself of one of the chains that bound him. To
Caroline Gordon, this is a serious misreading. "I suspect that Joyce's
Portrait has been misread by a whole generation." She sees the rejection as "the picture of a soul that is being damned for time and
eternity caught in the act of foreseeing and foreknowing its damnation," and she cites in evidence the fall of Icarus and Stephen's own
statement to Cranly that he is not afraid to make a mistake, "even
a great mistake, a lifelong mistake and perhaps for eternity, too." [5]
Well, which *Portrait* do we choose, that of the artistic soul battling
through successfully to his necessary freedom, or that of the child of
God, choosing, like Lucifer, his own damnation? No two books could
be further from each other than the two we envision here. There
may be a sufficient core of what is simply interesting to salvage the
book as a great work of the sensibility, but unless we are willing to
retreat into babbling and incommunicable relativism, we cannot believe that it is *both* a portrait of the prisoner freed *and* a portrait
of the soul placing itself in chains.

Critics have had even more difficulty with Stephen's aesthetic theory,

[3] *James Joyce* (Norfolk, Va., 1941), pp. 58–62.
[4] "Technique as Discovery," *Hudson Review*, I (Spring, 1948), 79–80.
[5] *How To Read a Novel* (New York, 1957), p. 213.

ostensibly developed from Aquinas. Is the book itself, as Grant Redford tells us,[6] an "objectification of an artistic proposition and a method announced by the central character," achieving for Joyce the "wholeness, harmony, and radiance" that Stephen celebrates in his theory? Or is it, as Father Noon says, an ironic portrait of Stephen's immature aesthetics? Joyce wanted to qualify Stephen's utterances, Father Noon tells us, "by inviting attention to his own more sophisticated literary concerns," and he stands apart from the Thomist aesthetics, watching Stephen miss the clue in his drive for an impersonal, dramatic narration. "The comparison of the artist with the God of the creation," taken "straight" by many critics, is for Father Noon "the climax of Joyce's ironic development of the Dedalus aesthetic." [7]

Finally, what of the precious villanelle? Does Joyce intend it to be taken as a serious sign of Stephen's artistry, as a sign of his genuine but amusingly pretentious precocity, or as something else entirely?

> Are you not weary of ardent ways,
> Lure of the fallen seraphim?
> Tell no more of enchanted days.
>
> Your eyes have set man's heart ablaze
> And you have had your will of him.
> Are you not weary of ardent ways? . . .

Hardly anyone has committed himself in public about the quality of this poem. Are we to smile at Stephen or pity him in his tortured longing? Are we to marvel at his artistry, or scoff at his conceit? Or are we merely to say, "How remarkable an insight into the kind of poem that would be written by an adolescent in love, if he were artistically inclined?" The poem, we are told, "enfolded him like a shining cloud, enfolded him like water with a liquid life: and like a cloud of vapour or like waters circumfluent in space the liquid letters of speech, symbols of the element of mystery, flowed forth over his brain." As we recall Jean Paul's formula for "romantic irony," "hot baths of sentiment followed by cold showers of irony," we can only ask here which tap has been turned on. Are we to swoon—or laugh?

Some critics will no doubt answer that all these questions are irrelevant. The villanelle is not to be judged but simply experienced; the aesthetic theory is, within the art work, neither true nor false but simply "true" to the art work—that is, true to Stephen's char-

---

[6] "The Role of Structure in Joyce's 'Portrait,'" *Modern Fiction Studies*, IV (Spring, 1958), 30. See also Herbert Gorman, *James Joyce* (London, 1941), p. 96, and Stuart Gilbert, *James Joyce's Ulysses* (London, 1930), pp. 20–22.

[7] William T. Noon, S.J., *Joyce and Aquinas* (New Haven, Conn., 1957), pp. 34, 35, 66, 67. See also Hugh Kenner, "The *Portrait* in Perspective," [reprinted above, pp. 26–37—Ed.]

acter at this point. To read modern literature properly we must re-
fuse to ask irrelevant questions about it; we must accept the "portrait" and no more ask whether the character portrayed is good or
bad, right or wrong than we ask whether a woman painted by Picasso
is moral or immoral. "All facts of any kind," as Gilbert puts it,
"mental or material, sublime or ludicrous, have an equivalence of
value for the artist." [8]

This answer, which can be liberating at one stage of our development in appreciating not only modern but all art, becomes less and
less satisfactory the longer we look at it. It certainly does not seem
to have been Joyce's basic attitude, though he was often misleading
about it.[9] The creation and the enjoyment of art can never be a
completely neutral activity. Though different works of art require
different kinds of judgment for their enjoyment, the position taken
in chapters three through five must stand: no work, not even the
shortest lyric, can be written in complete moral, intellectual and
aesthetic neutrality. We may judge falsely, we may judge uncon-
sciously, but we cannot even bring the book to mind without judging its elements, seeing them as shaped into a given kind of thing.
Even if we denied that the sequence of events has meaning in the
sense of being truly sequential, that denial would itself be a judgment on the rightness of Stephen's actions and opinions at each stage:
to decide that he is not growing is as much a judgment on his actions
as to decide that he is becoming more and more mature. Actually
everyone reads the book as some kind of progressive sequence, and
to do so we judge succeeding actions and opinions to be more or less
moral, sensitive, intellectually mature, than those they follow.[10] If we
felt that the question of Joyce's precise attitude toward Stephen's
vocation, his aesthetics, and his villanelle were irrelevant, we would
hardly dispute with each other about them. Yet I count in a recent
check list at least fifteen articles and one full book disputing Joyce's
attitude about the aesthetics alone.[11]

Like most modern critics, I would prefer to settle such disputes
by using internal rather than external evidence. But the experts themselves give me little hope of finding answers to my three problems by
re-reading *Portrait* one more time. They all clutch happily at any

[8] *James Joyce's Ulysses*, p. 22.

[9] Richard Ellmann concludes that whether we know it or not, "Joyce's court is,
like Dante's or Tolstoy's, always in session" (*James Joyce* [New York, 1959], p. 3).

[10] Norman Friedman considers it a "tribute to Joyce's dramatic genius that a Catholic can sympathize with the portrayal of Catholic values in the novel which the hero
rejects" ("Point of View in Fiction," *PMLA*, LXX [December, 1955], 11–84). But
this is not to say that the Catholic readers are right, or that we need not make up
our minds about the question.

[11] *Modern Fiction Studies*, IV (Spring, 1958), 72–99.

wisp of comment or fragmentary document that might illuminate Joyce's intentions.[12] And who can blame them?

The truth seems to be that Joyce was always a bit uncertain about his attitude toward Stephen. Anyone who reads Ellmann's masterful biography with this problem in mind cannot help being struck by the many shifts and turns Joyce took as he worked through the various versions. There is nothing especially strange in that, of course. Most "autobiographical" novelists probably encounter difficulty in trying to decide just how heroic their heroes are to be. But Joyce's explorations came just at a time when the traditional devices for control of distance were being repudiated, when doctrines of objectivity were in the air, and when people were taking seriously the idea that to evoke "reality" was a sufficient aim in art; the artist need not concern himself with judging or with specifying whether the reader should approve or disapprove, laugh or cry.

Now the traditional forms *had* specified in their very conceptions a certain degree of clarity about distance. If an author chose to write comedy, for example, he knew that his characters must at least to some degree be "placed" at a distance from the spectator's norms. This predetermination did not, of course, settle all of his problems. To balance sympathy and antipathy, admiration and contempt, was still a fundamental challenge, but it was a challenge for which there was considerable guidance in the practice of previous writers of comedy. If, on the other hand, he chose to write tragedy, or satire, or elegy, or celebration odes, or whatever, he could rely to some extent on conventions to guide him and his audience to a common attitude toward his characters.

The young Joyce had none of this to rely on, but he seems never to have sensed the full danger of his position. When, in his earliest years, he recorded his brief epiphanies—those bits of dialogue or description that were supposed to reveal the inner reality of things—there was always an implied identification of the recorder's norms and the reader's; both were spectators at the revealing moment, both shared in the vision of one moment of truth. Though some of the epiphanies are funny, some sad, and some mixed, the basic effect is always the same: an overwhelming sense—when they succeed—of what Joyce liked to call the "incarnation": Artistic Meaning has come to live in the world's body. The Poet has done his work.

Even in these early epiphanies there is difficulty with distance; the author inevitably expects the reader to share in his own preconceptions and interests sufficiently to catch, from each word or gesture,

[12] See, for example, J. Mitchell Morse's defense of a fairly "straight" reading of *Ulysses*, based largely on Gorman's reading of Joyce's *Notebooks* ("Augustine, *Ayenbite*, and *Ulysses*," *PMLA*, LXX (December, 1955), 1147, n. 12.

the precise mood or tone that they evoke for the author himself. But since complete identification with the author is a silent precondition for the success of such moments, the basic problem of distance is never a serious one. Even if the author and reader should differ in interpretation, they can share the sense of evoked reality.

It is only when Joyce places at the center of a long work a figure who experiences epiphanies, an epiphany-producing device, as it were, who is himself used by the real author as an object ambiguously distant from the norms of the work, that the complications of distance become incalculable. If he treats the author-figure satirically, as he does in much of *Stephen Hero*, that earlier, windier version of *Portrait*,[13] then what happens to the quality of the epiphanies that *he* describes? Are they still genuine epiphanies or only what the misguided, callow youth *thinks* are epiphanies? If, as Joyce's brother Stanislaus has revealed, the word "hero" is satiric, can we take seriously that anti-hero's vision? Yet if the satirical mode is dropped, if the hero is made into a real hero, and if the reader is made to see things entirely as he sees them, what then happens to objectivity? The portrait is no longer an objective rendering of reality, looked at from a respectable aesthetic distance, but rather a mere subjective indulgence.

Joyce can be seen, in Ellmann's account, wrestling with this problem throughout the revisions. Unlike writers before Flaubert, he had no guidance from convention or tradition or fellow artists. Neither Flaubert nor James had established any sure ground to stand on. Both of them had, in fact, stumbled on the same hurdles, and though each had on occasion surmounted the difficulties, Joyce was in no frame of mind to look behind their claims as realists to the actual problems and lessons that lay beneath their evocative surfaces. A supreme egoist struggling to deal artistically with his own ego, a humorist who could not escape the comic consequences of his portrait of that inflated ego, he faced, in the completed *Stephen Hero*, what he had to recognize as a hodge-podge of irreconcilables. Is Stephen a pompous ass or not? Is his name deliberately ridiculous, as Stanislaus, who invented it, says? Or is it a serious act of symbolism? The way out seems inevitable, but it seems a retreat nonetheless: simply present the "reality" and let the reader judge. Cut all the author's judgments, cut all of the adjectives, produce one long, ambiguous epiphany.[14]

[13] Ed. Theodore Spencer, 1944. Only part of the MS survives.
[14] See Denis Donoghue's "Joyce and the Finite Order," *Sewanee Review*, LXVIII (Spring, 1960), 256–73: "The objects [in *Portrait*] exist to provide a suitably piteous setting for Stephen as Sensitive Plant; they are meant to mark a sequence of experiences in the mode of *pathos*. . . . The lyric situation is insulated from probes, and there is far too much of this cosseting in the *Portrait*. . . . Drama or rhetoric should have warned Joyce that Stephen the aesthetic *alazon* needed nothing so ur-

Purged of the author's explicit judgment, the resulting work was so brilliant and compelling, its hero's vision so scintillating, that almost all readers overlooked the satiric and ironic content—except, of course, as the satire operated against *other* characters. So far as I know no one said anything about irony against Stephen until after *Ulysses* was published in 1922, with its opening in which Icarus–Stephen is shown with his wings clipped. Ironic readings did not become popular, in fact, until after the fragment of *Stephen Hero* was published in 1944. Readers of that work found, it is true, many authoritative confirmations of their exaltation of Stephen—for the most part in a form that might confirm anyone's prejudice against commentary. ". . . When he [Stephen] wrote it was always a mature and reasoned emotion which urged him" [*SH*, 174]. "This mood of indignation which was not guiltless of a certain superficiality was undoubtedly due to the excitement of release. . . . He acknowledged to himself in honest egoism that he could not take to heart the distress of a nation, the soul of which was antipathetic to his own, so bitterly as the indignity of a bad line of verse: but at the same time he was nothing in the world so little as an amateur artist" [*SH*, 146]. "Stephen did not attach himself to art in any spirit of youthful dilettantism but strove to pierce to the significant heart of everything" [*SH*, 33]. But readers were also faced with a good many denigrations of the hero. We can agree that *Portrait* is a better work because the immature author has been effaced; Joyce may indeed have found that effacing the commentary was the only way he could obtain an air of maturity. But the fact remains that it is primarily to this immature commentary that we must go for evidence in deciphering the ironies of the later, purer work.

What we find in *Stephen Hero* is not a simple confirmation of any reading that we might have achieved on the basis of *Portrait* alone. Rather we find an extremely complicated view, combining irony and admiration in unpredictable mixtures. Thus the Thomist aesthetics "was in the main applied Aquinas and he set it forth plainly with a naif air of discovering novelties. This he did partly to satisfy his own taste for enigmatic roles and partly from a genuine predisposition in favour of all but the premises of scholasticism" [*SH*, 77]. No one ever inferred, before this passage was available, anything like this precise and complex judgment on Stephen. The combination of blame and approval, we may be sure, is different in the finished *Portrait*; the implied author no doubt often repudiates the explicit judgments of the younger narrator who intrudes into *Stephen*

---

gently as a correspondingly deft *eiron;* lacking this, the book is blind in one eye" (p. 258). Joyce would no doubt reply—I think unfairly—that he intended Stephen as both *alazon* and *eiron.*

Hero. But we can also be sure that his judgment has not become less complex. Where do we find, in any criticism of *Portrait* based entirely on internal evidence, the following kind of juxtaposition of Stephen's views with the author's superior insight? "Having by this *simple process* established the literary form of art as the most excellent he *proceeded to examine it in favour of his theory*, or *as he rendered it*, to establish the relations which must subsist between the literary image, the work of art itself, and that energy which had imagined and fashioned it, that center of conscious, re-acting, particular life, the artist" ([*SH*, 77]; italics mine). Can we infer, from *Portrait*, that Joyce sees Stephen as simply rationalizing in favor of his theory? Did we guess that Joyce could refer to him mockingly as a "fiery-hearted revolutionary" and a "heaven-ascending essayist"? [15]

In *Stephen Hero*, the author's final evaluation of the aesthetics is favourable but qualified: "Except for the eloquent and arrogant peroration Stephen's essay was a careful exposition of a carefully meditated theory of esthetic" [*SH*, 80–81]. Though it might be argued that in the finished book he has cut out some of the negative elements, such as the "eloquent and arrogant peroration," and has presented the pure theory in conversational form, it is clear that Joyce himself judged his hero's theory in greater detail than we could possibly infer from the final version alone.

Similar clarifications can be found in *Stephen Hero* of our other two crucial problems, his rejection of the priesthood and his poetic

---

[15] One reviewer of *Stephen Hero* was puzzled to notice in it that the omniscient author, not yet purged in accordance with Joyce's theories of dramatic narration, frequently expresses biting criticism of the young Stephen. The earlier work thus seemed to him "much more cynical," and "much, much farther from the principles of detached classicism that had been formulated before either book was written." How could the man who wrote *Stephen Hero* go on and write, "in a mood of enraptured fervour," a work like *Portrait?*" (*T.L.S.*, February 1, 1957, p. 64).

It is true that, once we have been alerted, signs of ironic intention come rushing to our view. Those of us who now believe that Joyce is not entirely serious in the passages on aesthetics must wonder, for example, how we ever read them "straight." What did we make out of passages like the following, in those old, benighted days before we saw what was going on? "The lore which he was believed to pass his days brooding upon so that it had rapt him from the companionship of youth was only a garner of slender sentences from Aristotle's Poetics and Psychology and a *Synopsis Philosophiæ Scholasticæ ad mentem divi Thomæ*. His thinking was a dusk of doubt and selfmistrust, lit up at moments by the lightnings of intuition. . . ." "In those moments the world perished about his feet as if it had been [with] fire consumed: and thereafter his tongue grew heavy and he met the eyes of others with unanswering eyes for he felt that the spirit of beauty had folded him round like a mantle and that in reverie at least he had been acquainted with nobility. But, when this brief pride of silence upheld him no longer, he was glad to find himself still in the midst of common lives, passing on his way amid the squalor and noise and sloth of the city fearlessly and with a light heart" (opening pp. of chap. v). If this is not mockery, however tender, it is fustian.

ability. For example, "He had swept the moment into his memory . . . and . . . had brought forth some pages of sorry verse" [*SH*, 67]. Can the hero of *Portrait* be thought of as writing "sorry verse"? One would not think so, to read much of the commentary by Joyce's critics.

But who is to blame them? Whatever intelligence Joyce postulates in his reader—let us assume the unlikely case of its being comparable to his own—will not be sufficient for precise inference of a pattern of judgments which is, after all, private to Joyce. And this will be true regardless of how much distance from his own hero we believe him to have achieved by the time he concluded his final version. We simply cannot avoid the conclusion that to some extent the book itself is at fault, regardless of its great virtues. Unless we make the absurd assumption that Joyce had in reality purged himself of all judgment by the time he completed his final draft, unless we see him as having really come to look upon all of Stephen's actions as equally wise or equally foolish, equally sensitive or equally meaningless, we must conclude that many of the refinements he intended in his finished *Portrait* are, for most of us, permanently lost. Even if we were now to do our homework like dutiful students, even if we were to study all of Joyce's work, even if we were to spend the lifetime that Joyce playfully said his novels demand, presumably we should never come to as rich, as refined, and as varied a conception of the quality of Stephen's last days in Ireland as Joyce had in mind. For some of us the air of detachment and objectivity may still be worth the price, but we must never pretend that a price was not paid.

Irony in Joyce's *Portrait:*
The Stasis of Pity

by F. Parvin Sharpless

Irony, it has been recently observed, has replaced the symbol as the primary quarry of the close reader.[1] One of the most elusive and slippery instances of this prey is the question of the consistency, scope, intensity, and tone of the irony directed toward Stephen Dedalus in Joyce's *A Portrait of the Artist as a Young Man.* The determination of appropriate terms for judgments of Stephen's various stages of growth is a vexing one, affording a wide range of possibilities. To draw the extremes, Stephen may be seen as a courageous artist-hero, casting off the forms and conventions of society as inappropriate to his gifts and destiny, freeing himself to soar away from Ireland to a fulfillment of his mission as a fabulous Dedalian artificer; or, Stephen may be seen as a callow and affected poseur, a "farcical pedagogue," a morbidly sensitive pseudo-artist, whose literary theory is weak Thomism, and whose literary practise a faded aestheticism. In recent years a number of critics have begun to move beyond this simple polarity, suggesting that clear and emphatic judgments of this kind are not proper to the distinctive nature of Joyce's art. Hugh Kenner makes the point clearly by observing that Joyce's interest is "not dramatically to 'place' Stephen but to reveal his lyric reality; to invite an apprehension, not a judgment." [2] But neither Kenner's discussion, nor those of Wayne C. Booth and Robert E. Scholes, are able to sustain the theoretical objectivity which the latter two follow Kenner in approving. Kenner himself is exasperated by the

[1] Edward H. Rosenberry, "The Problem of *Billy Budd,*" *PMLA,* LXXX (December 1965), 490.

[2] Hugh Kenner, *Dublin's Joyce* (Boston, 1962), p. 99. The last pages, Kenner adds, are "painful reading" because of Joyce's unresolved "moral ambiguity" toward Stephen (p. 121).

Stephen of chapter V over whom he exercises a quite severe judgment, calling him an unregenerate aesthete, "humourless" and "priggish," "who cannot remember what day of the week it is, [who] sentimentalizes like Charles Lamb over the 'human pages' of a secondhand Latin book, conducts the inhumanly pedantic dialogue with Cranly on mother-love, writes Frenchified verses in bed in an erotic swoon, and is epiphanized at full length, like Shem the Penman beneath the bedclothes, shrinking from the 'common noises' of daylight." [3] Scholes likes Stephen a little and Stephen's villanelle a lot and therefore argues that "we must make allowances for a certain amount of callowness in the protagonist." [4] Booth recognizes ambiguity in the portrait of Stephen but concludes that Joyce's attempt to allow the reader to apprehend rather than judge is a failure.

> We simply cannot avoid the conclusion that to some extent the book itself is at fault, regardless of its great virtues. Unless we make the absurd assumption that Joyce had in reality purged himself of all judgment [of the protagonist] by the time he had completed his final draft, unless we see him as having really come to look upon all of Stephen's actions as equally wise or equally foolish, equally sensitive or equally meaningless, we must conclude that many of the refinements he intended in his finished *Portrait* are, for most of us, permanently lost.[5]

This view gives us a difficult choice: either the novel is flawed by Joyce's failure to provide adequate means by which the reader may judge Stephen (as Booth thinks because Joyce himself could not achieve sufficient clarity of judgment) or, what is worse, the novel is flawed by a "babbling and incommunicable relativism" [6] in which the reader may see and judge Stephen in any light and by any standard he wishes.

There is no doubt that the special techniques of the novel—the rigorous exclusion of authorial "presence" either explicit or implicit, and the consequent absence of any means of directly controlling the reader's response—do invite these mistakes. The 'point of view' of *A Portrait* represents only the exclusive subjectivity of the protagonist, a subjectivity, moreover, which itself is in motion through time in a way that requires it to reflect even its subjectivity differently from one moment to the next.[7] But the judgments which these techniques

[3] Kenner, p. 112.

[4] Robert E. Scholes, "Stephen Dedalus: *Eiron* and *Alazon*," *Studies in Literature and Language*, III (Spring 1961), 12.

[5] Wayne C. Booth, *The Rhetoric of Fiction* (Chicago, 1961), pp. 335–336. [See this volume p. 95—ED.]

[6] Booth, p. 328. [See this volume p. 88—ED.]

[7] This aspect of much modern fiction, discussed by Booth, is noted in the discussion of *A Portrait* by Dorothy Van Ghent, *The English Novel, Form and Function* (New York, 1953), p. 267.

deny us are those which Stephen would call "kinetic," that is, they
are subjective, involved, and active, they are the kind of affective
apprehension coloring Kenner's hostility, and they are of the kind
that Stephen's theoretical classicism given in chapter V rules out as
an inappropriate critical stance.[8] The better choice is to adopt the
attitude which Kenner recommends without following, that of appre-
hending without judgment, of substituting for kinetic response a special kind of static apprehension in which the clarity, radiance, and
harmony of the object, its particular *quidditas*, become the essential
constituents of the aesthetic experience.

The particular attitude which is thus created in Joyce's works has
been excellently described by S. L. Goldberg, who terms it "Classical."

> In very broad terms, we may say that, as Joyce understood the term, the
> classical temper is essentially dramatic. It accepts the ordinary world of
> humanity as the primary object of its attention, and endeavours to see it
> and present it steadily and whole. In order to do so, it seeks patiently
> for maturity, detachment, impersonality of judgment, and an artistic
> method, that, while it begins with the local and the concrete as its
> foundation, enables it to penetrate beyond them.[9]

Applied to Stephen Dedalus this view allows a much richer and more
complex irony than is usually recognized under the term, and, more
important, it removes the necessity of judging the protagonist in
simple alternatives, calling instead for static apprehension, rather
than kinetic judgment. We can, under this aspect, see Stephen as
wise *and* foolish, callow *and* mature; we can see his actions as "true"
in the formal sense to his condition. Joyce's irony, as Goldberg puts
it, does not "dissolve" its object. Rather it is a "qualifying criticism,
which does not imply a total rejection of its object in the least. Irony
and sympathetic understanding, or even love, are not necessarily incom-
patible, nor is there any reason why Stephen's potentialities as an
artist should be dismissed because he is very immature and clearly
portrayed as such." [10]

Although this is the proper way to defend the novel, it is a defense
which places a great burden on the reader, by requiring of him a
breadth of insight, a maturity, a wholeness of vision as great as that
of the artist, and of a kind that few critics have shown themselves
capable of sustaining to the end of *A Portrait*. But instead of finding the cause of this difficulty in Joyce's faulty control of his subject matter, we can more confidently find the reason in the fact that
the early chapters deal with issues and values which are sufficiently
childish, sufficiently distant from adult kinetic involvement as to

---

[8] Pp. 204–215.
[9] S. L. Goldberg, *The Classical Temper: a Study of "Ulysses"* (London, 1961), p. 32.
[10] Goldberg, p. 110.

make detachment and classical stasis easy to achieve. But as Stephen's world enlarges, the import, the kinetic potential of the experiences increases and their distance from the reader's subjectivity decreases. It is likely then that at some point the relation between Stephen and the reader will change from static to kinetic, and at this point we will either call Stephen a prig, or conclude that Joyce's control of the irony is false and clumsy, when in fact it is our own failure to recognize that the kinetic subjectivity is not in the work but in our minds.

The matter is easy to illustrate. What is the proper response on the part of the reader to the unjust punishment of Stephen by Father Dolan? The incident will support either of two kinetic responses. Because one hates tyrannical authority the reader may be filled with outrage against Father Dolan, and be suffused with satisfaction at the success of Stephen's visit to Father Conmee; he can, in short, feel as deeply moved by the incident as Stephen himself. If so, it follows that Stephen will be judged as a hero, and the meaning of the incident will be taken to presage later triumphs of artistic individuality over the ignorance and corruption of institutions, and to show that priests should not be suffered to contain that ambition. But, on the other hand, if one hates revolutions, violations of order, going out of channels, if one dislikes particularly little boys who don't know *their* places, then the reader will conclude that Joyce is directing irony against Stephen's youth, his independence, his pride, his belief in himself, his confidence in his ability to win freedom. It is safe to say that few readers are likely to find in this experience ground for either of such elaborate kinetic responses. One at once recognizes the objective *quidditas* of the situation as one appropriate to Stephen at his age and given his particular character. One recognizes the formal relationship of this event to Stephen's future, as thematically proper for one who will continue to distrust authority, and this recognition does not involve a judgment of whether Stephen is right or wrong in being this kind of person. In a larger sense, we have made our own peace with this kind of experience. True, we say, one's first experience of injustice is traumatic and painful, but one learns, one accepts, one achieves objectivity, even toward the failings of one's old teachers. From where *we* stand, the way of the world does not make one pandying cause for weeping.[11]

Similarly other incidents in the early chapters are easily seen for their *quidditas,* the irony always qualifying, never judging absolutely.

[11] Yet at the same time the incident is not pathetic. Although Stephen does not know enough of the world to recognize the insignificance of the incident, he is right to recognize the injustice. Kinetic response would certainly occur in a reader were Stephen to thank Father Dolan for his correction, admitting that he should have endeavored not to break his glasses.

Stephen's sufferings during the political argument on Christmas Day, the sentimental vision of Monte Cristo's Mercedes, his imagined rejection of her too late offered love ("Madame, I never eat muscatel grapes" [63]), are all seen with the same objective double vision: the sanctity of parental authority, the ideal purity of adolescent love are not false, and to believe in them at an appropriate time in life is only to be a child. But they are situations and conditions from which further experience and time have insulated and separated us; we look with objective detachment on innocences from which we have fallen. But as Stephen grows older the questions become more difficult as their content comes closer to the area of the reader's unobjectified experience. Yet the reader is asked to maintain the same objectivity over Stephen's sexual experiences, his struggles with sin and with the church, with his family and with God. We can no more conclude that Stephen is a fool for rejecting the ordered disciplined life for bohemian nonconformity than we can conclude in the earlier case that his fear of being pandied is foolish or overly-sensitive. If we do make such judgments, it is because we have not yet reached sufficient degree of detachment for ourselves in relation to the particular subject.[12]

Joyce's classicism sees all aspects of human life as meaningful and absurd at the same time. This is true even of things which he might be expected to value most: the creative process of the literary artist. Yet even here the same objectivity and qualifying irony prevail. This is particularly difficult for critics who take Joyce's work very seriously to understand. Thus Scholes, in a recent discussion, gives an admirable reading of Stephen's villanelle, and concludes that because the poem is able to sustain a complex exegesis, "there is no hint of mockery in Joyce's reverent attitude toward the creative process." [13] It is, however, always dangerous to read Joyce without awareness of this qualifying contrapuntal irony, abundantly present in the account of the composition of the villanelle by dawn's early light. Indeed, here we find the technique in its commonest form: the juxtaposition of a moment of exalted, serious vision, with matter of a lower kind. Thus Stephen's vision of the seraphic beauty is counterpointed with uncomfortably terrestrial interpolations: the exaggerated Paterian setting, the coarse and unpoetic associations ("ellipsoidal ball"! [218]), jealousy of Father Moran (221), the "great overblown flowers of the tattered wallpaper" (221–222). But this counterpoint does not mean that Stephen is a fool,

---

[12] Almost all kinetic responses are the product of a reader valuing an idea or experience apart from its balancing opposite, of forgetting on individual issues, the ironic commentary, which, in classicism, is always possible and necessary. Usually, and in Joyce always, kinesis is in the mind of the beholder.

[13] Robert E. Scholes, "Stephen Dedalus, Poet or Esthete?" *PMLA*, LXXIX (September 1964), 484–489.

nor that his villanelle lacks merit. What it does provide is an alterative
and corrective view to Stephen's. Moreover, Joyce was quite capable
of taking the same double view of his own artistic practice. Describing
the structural principles of the *Oxen of the Sun* section of *Ulysses*,
Joyce concludes with a reversal of tone which qualifies but does not
refute the seriousness of what has gone before.

> This procession is also linked back at each part subtly with some fore-
> going episode of the day and, besides this, with the natural stages of
> development in the embryo and the periods of faunal evolution in gen-
> eral. The double-thudding Anglo-Saxon motive recurs from time to time
> ("Loth to move from Horne's house") to give the sense of the hoofs of
> oxen. Bloom is the spermatozoon, the hospital the womb, the nurse the
> ovum, Stephen the embryo.
> How's that for high? [14]

It seems best to consider the novel in such a way as to allow one
critical stance to be maintained throughout. The uncertainty and
controversy which various contrasting judgments of Stephen have
raised do not suggest authorial error or unsureness as much they
indicate a novel requiring greater objectivity than most readers can
manage. But even this objection goes only against the theory, not
its execution. Finally, we may admit that the classicism which seems
to be at work here is, as Booth says, relativistic. It is not a relativism
which is "babbling and incoherent" but one shaped by the only
absolute that this view has available—the existence in the artistic
rendering of the real matter of the world of an essential *quidditas,*
inherent in these objects and capable of being isolated and shown
through (epiphanized) their envelope of sensory material. But perception of this absolute stasis is possible only after the reader has
cleared his own vision of its subjective and relativistic kineticisms.[15]

II

Since Stephen is striving to become an artist, his progress or lack
of it toward this goal can be measured by the degree to which he
is able to overcome kinetic responses and achieve classical stasis. Indeed the main "plot" or action of the novel may be said to lie in
Stephen's movement from kinetic involvement with various people
and institutions, his family, friends, with priests, the church, his
country, to a state of objective detachment toward them. In this

---

[14] *Letters of James Joyce,* ed. Stuart Gilbert (New York, 1957), p. 139.

[15] When Stephen in *Ulysses* complains about the nightmare of history and the
"ineluctable modality of the visible" he is reflecting his fear of relativity of subjective perception as the antithesis of art.

movement one can trace three stages or levels. In the earliest, most youthful stage, Stephen's commitments are deeply felt and overwhelming to the personality. They are usually accompanied by public humiliation and with painful retreats which require the thematic apologies which Stephen finds so difficult. The second stage finds Stephen still responding with a degree of involvement, but able to conceal any overt show of the depth of his response, thus protecting himself from public shame. In this stage his exterior manner becomes a form which controls the emotion, a suitable classical stance. Finally, in some areas, he reaches objective stasis, looking on the object of his previous emotion with a detached and complex irony, one of the primary qualities of which is pity.

Illustrations of this sequence can be made by tracing almost any of the primary relationships of Stephen's life, but it is perhaps clearest in his experiences with priests and with E. C. (Emma Clery). In the encounter with Father Dolan in chapter I, Stephen's kinetic involvement is evident enough, both in his pain and humiliation at his punishment ("the scalding water burst forth from his eyes and, burning with shame and agony and fear, he drew back his shaking arm in terror and burst out into a whine of pain" [51]), and in his pride at gaining redress from Father Conmee ("He was alone. He was happy and free: but he would not be anyway proud with Father Dolan" [59]). Stephen's next encounter with priestly authority is also recalled with pain: the public rebuke for having "heresy in his essay" (79). But by the time Stephen is approached by the director of the Jesuit order with the suggestion that he consider whether he is called to the priesthood (153–160), he has learned, not detachment, but a measure of concealment and control which protects his emotions from the world's sight.

This is the more impressive in view of the subtlety of the psychological strategems employed against him by the priest. The scene is arranged as for an interrogation. The priest stands with his back to the light allowing him to search Stephen's face in the full light of the declining afternoon sun. The priest begins the conversation by suggesting in an oblique fashion the superiority of the Jesuit order to the Dominican, Franciscan, and Capuchin, alluding playfully to the Capuchin's voluminous cassock, and implying that it is a bit old-fashioned and in contrast to the more worldly and progressive Jesuit garb. Stephen, we may assume, is not accustomed to being admitted to this degree of familiarity, and the intention of the remark is not only to reflect the superiority of the Society of Jesus, but to create a subtle flattery of Stephen by treating him to an extent as an equal. But Stephen is careful not to express any opinion on the question of monkish dress. When the director refers to difficulties that the Capuchins have riding bicycles, Stephen agrees: "It must be

troublesome, I imagine?" The director then with ostensible casual-
ness refers to the garments by the slang name they are given in Belgium: "les jupes." The word (sometimes "jupon" or "jupe de dessous")
in its simplest sense means "skirt" or "petticoat," but its connotations
can be erotic, suggesting fetishistic responses.[16] But Stephen is on
guard, and avoids the two traps that have been laid for him: he does
not join in the facetious criticism of the Capuchin order, nor does he
allow his face or manner to show that he has ever heard or thought
about women's underwear, even though "the names of articles of
dress worn by women or of certain soft and delicate stuffs used in their
making brought always to his mind a delicate and sinful perfume."
(155)

The basis of Stephen's success in this situation is his awareness of
the gestures of the director as detached from their true motives. Seeing
the priests's word as "disingenuous," seeing them as part of a pre-
conceived performance, is to provide the objectifying distance which
is a step in the direction of stasis. Here he does not (as he later finds
possible) counter the director's maneuvers with superior moves of
his own, but he can assume a polite, defensive caution, by which his
own emotion is concealed and controlled.

The final stage is even greater detachment in which the dean of
studies of University College is acted upon by Stephen's own conscious gestures. Here the distance between them, the degree of objectivity, is so great as to wipe out all Stephen's kinetic feeling, re-
placing it with "desolating pity." (184ff.) The dean clumsily tries to
warn Stephen against free thinking:

> These questions are very profound, Mr Dedalus, said the dean. It is like
> looking down from the cliffs of Moher into the depths. Many go down
> into the depths and never come up. Only the trained diver can go down
> into those depths and explore them and come to the surface again. (187)

Stephen parries the warning with pious quotations from Aristotle and
Aquinas. He then unintentionally confuses and embarrasses the dean
by quoting from Newman, and then confounds him further on the
subject of tundishes. Suddenly these incidents, plus the dean's English
accent, strike Stephen in a new way, and bring a new emotion into
his mind.

> A desolating pity began to fall like a dew upon his easily embittered
> heart for this faithful servingman of the knightly Loyola, for this half-
> brother of the clergy, more venal than they in speech, more steadfast of

---

[16] Delicately: "la partie de l'habillement des femmes qui descend depuis la cein-
ture jusqu'aux pieds." The more picturesque sense is present in this passage from
Gautier: "Quand de sa jupe qui tourn / Elle souleve le volant, / Sa jambe, sous le
bas de soie / Prend des lueurs de marbre blanc." Stephen may have been reading
even worse stuff.

soul than they, one whom he would never call his ghostly father: and he thought how this man and his companions had earned the name of worldlings at the hands not of the unworldly only but of the worldly also for having pleaded, during all their history, at the bar of God's justice for the souls of the lax and the lukewarm and the prudent. (190)

The problem of the church in general and the authority of priests in particular is thus "solved" by Stephen's insight and equanimity. His greater quickness of mind, his consciousness of the dean's gestures as gestures, his consciousness of the failure of the man to achieve the visionary ideal which he pursues, all combine to drain Stephen of kinetic emotion. He passes beyond concern with the issue as issue. Bitterness is replaced by pity, alien, objective, and sad. The dean, being no longer an object in life, is ready to become an object in art.

A similar progression, more painfully won, can be traced in the case of Stephen's relations with E. C. (Emma Clery). Standing with her on the steps of the tramcar "his heart danced upon her movements like a cork upon a tide." (69) Later, failing to kiss her, he sits alone in the car tearing his ticket to shreds and staring gloomily at the floor (70). But by the time of the Whitsuntide play these kinetic feelings are only momentary and are concealed from the world. He disguises the "shaft of momentary anger" which he feels at Heron's "indelicate" "I wouldn't care a bit, by Jove, she's ripping, isn't she, Wallis?" (77) Now, even though he has been filled all day with "restless moodiness" at the prospect of the evening encounter, "the adventure in his mind stood in no danger from their words; and his face mirrored his rival's false smile." (78) As with the director, Stephen affects an external manner which protects the inner emotion by repeating facetiously the Confiteor. Artifice controls kinetic response. Thus "the episode ended well for both Heron and Wallis laughed indulgently at the irreverence." [17]

But this is objectivity in manner not in fact. The third stage is not managed until the Diary entry for April 15:

> Met her today pointblank in Grafton Street. The crowd brought us together. We both stopped. She asked me why I never came, said she had heard all sorts of stories about me. This was only to gain time. Asked me, was I writing poems? About whom? I asked her. This confused her more and I felt sorry and mean. Turned off that valve at once and opened the spiritual-heroic refrigerating apparatus, invented and patented in all countries by Dante Alighieri. Talked rapidly of myself and my plans. In the midst of it unluckily I made a sudden gesture of a revolutionary nature. I must have looked like a fellow throwing a hand-

---

[17] This contrast is emphasized by the juxtaposition of this incident in Stephen's memory with one on the Clonliffe Road where Stephen does not control his responses, and suffers a humiliating beating because of his too overt partisanship of Byron (80–82).

ful of peas into the air. People began to look at us. She shook hands a
moment after and, in going away, said she hoped I would do what I said.
Now I call that friendly, don't you? (252)

This passage illustrates the symptoms of detachment: Stephen first
recognizes her gesture of inquiry as a gesture designed to involve
him, as a flirtation, and to see it as such is to drain it of its effect,
and to distance the perceiver from the object. His response is a parry-
ing, but from superior strength which, as in the case of the dean of
studies, confuses its antagonist and causes Stephen to feel pity, the
final mark of the objective posture ("I felt sorry and mean"). Beyond
this, however, we have a new level, for here Stephen is beginning to
be consciously detached from his own gestures, his own behavior, seeing
the action of yesterday with the detachment of today.[18] At the end of
the Diary Stephen retains kinetic feelings only toward his Dedalean
destiny, and toward what he calls "life." But with the world, or most
of it, gone into the objective distance, the dialogue of the mind
with itself which Stephen carries on in *Ulysses* is about to begin.
Stephen is now able to make his life into art, but he is beginning to
be unable to live it.[19]

III

Our argument may be summarized and concluded by suggesting
the analogy of a series of concentric circles named after the list in

[18] Her embarrassment at his gesture is an appropriate termination of their relationship because it shows her particular weakness of spirit, and more generally the
domination of Irish womenhood by priests, which makes them fear the artist's
call to their batlike souls.

[19] The same progression from kinetic involvement through detachment to pity is
found in Stephen's feelings toward Wells who pushed the young boy into the ditch
because he would not trade his snuff box for Wells's seasoned hacking chestnut. This
is the last we hear of Wells in *A Portrait*, but *Stephen Hero* contains a passage
which reverses the earlier situation. Wells is now a seminarian and anxious to impress his former schoolmate; he makes gestures of status: remembering a message
he must give to the dean, condescending to other students. Stephen sees the gestures
as such and finds that with this perception his long-standing kinetic hatred has dissolved.

> As Stephen looked at the big vague block of masonry looming before them
> through the faint daylight, he re-entered again in thought the seminarist life
> which he had led for so many years to the understanding of the narrow ac-
> tivities to which he could now in a moment bring the spirit of an acute sym-
> pathetic alien.

(72–73)

As he leaves the cloister Stephen watches Wells run awkwardly up the drive and
smiles "at his own impulse of pity," a state which he considers a "ripeness," a
"mature" pleasure.

Stephen's school copybook: Class of Elements, Clongowes Wood College, Sallins, Country Kildare, Ireland, Europe, The World, The Universe. Time and experience have moved Stephen outward from circles of smaller diameter to ones of larger and larger dimensions, leaving him at the end of *A Portrait* somewhere between Ireland and Europe. Toward those areas of experience outside Stephen's level of development, Stephen remains kinetically involved. But more and more of life falls inside the circle, making both incident and individuals objects of pity, turning these materials into suitable forms for aesthetic ordering, by seeing them with objective pity and stasis.

The difficulty of accomplishing this cannot be overstated, nor can its dangers. Pity is an emotion which drains away kinetic passions which, while they may be painful, constitute the vital springs of the average sensual man's basic motivations, particularly his ability to relate to and love objects and people. Joyce undoubtedly recognized the dangers to the artist of this aesthetic. Being refined out of existence, as Stephen recommends for the artist, is a kind of death, a death in which the sensual reality becomes less and less real, falling contemplatively into a lifeless formality, like Yeats's Byzantium, where everything is perfect and passionless, where the bird sings only to a drowsy emperor and to bored lords and ladies looking on in objective detached stasis.

Joyce's antidote to this condition was of course Bloom. Stephen as proto-artist finds experience valuable as a source of aesthetic raw material, but this denies its common meaning. Bloom is not an artist and therefore has no purpose for experience except to be experienced. His pity for others is not alien and detached, but sympathetic and kinetic. His perceptions of reality, of people and things, draw him closer to them, and to the life that lies in them. This explains, perhaps, why *Ulysses* is a more attractive book, and accounts for the sort of objections that have been made to Stephen's personality. The reader, perhaps closer in his mode of experiencing life to Bloom than to Stephen, finds Bloom's sensibility richer and more attractive; the soul which shows through his reality is one which is moving toward a fullness of human experience as vital in itself.

PART TWO

View Points

Harry Levin

The *Künstlerroman* offered a tentative solution to the dilemma of Joyce's generation, by enabling writers to apply the methods of realism to the subject of art. It enabled Marcel Proust to communicate experience more fully and subtly than had been done before, because it was his own experience that he was communicating, and because he was an artist to his finger-tips. *A la recherche du temps perdu* has been described as a novel that was written to explain why it was written. But, having come to be written, it offers other novelists little stimulus toward self-portraiture. It is singularly fitting that *Ulysses* should have appeared in the year of Proust's death. The perverse logic of André Gide can still present, in his *Journal des faux-monnayeurs*, the diary of a novelist who is writing a novel about a novelist who is keeping a diary about the novel he is writing. Of course, the *Künstler-roman* has no logical limit; but, like the label on the box of Quaker Oats, it has a vanishing-point. Already it is beginning to look as old-fashioned as Murger's *Vie de Bohême*.

The *Künstlerroman*, though it reverses the more normal proce-dure of applying the methods of art to the subject of reality, is the only conception of the novel that is specialized enough to include *A Portrait of the Artist as a Young Man*. In 1913, the year before Joyce finished his book, D. H. Lawrence had published his own portrait of the artist, *Sons and Lovers*. Both books convey the claustral sense of a young intelligence swaddled in convention and constricted by poverty, and the intensity of its first responses to esthetic experience and life at large. The extent to which Lawrence warms to his theme is the measure of Joyce's reserve. Characteristically, they may be reacting from the very different institutions behind them—evangelical English protestantism and Irish Catholic orthodoxy—when Lawrence dwells on the attractions of life, and Joyce on its repulsions. The respective mothers of the two artists play a similar role, yet May Dedalus is a wraith beside the full-bodied realization of Mrs. Morel. The characters in *Sons and Lovers* seem to enjoy an independent existence; in the *Portrait of the Artist* they figure mainly in the hero's reveries and

From James Joyce, *by Harry Levin (New York: New Directions Publishing Cor-poration, 1960; London: Faber & Faber, Ltd., 1960), pp. 42–43. Copyright 1941, © 1960 by New Directions Publishing Corporation. Reprinted by permission of the author, New Directions Publishing Corporation, and Faber & Faber, Ltd.*

resentments. Joyce's treatment of childhood is unrelieved in its sadness: endless generations of choirs of children sounded, for Stephen Dedalus, the same note of pain and weariness that Newman had heard in Vergil. "All seemed weary of life even before entering upon it." [164]

Eugene M. Waith

Stephen Dedalus as he appears in *A Portrait of the Artist as a Young Man* is far from being a godlike hero. Groping painfully toward some understanding of himself and his place in the world, he is sometimes laughable, sometimes pathetic, and nearly always what we should call "difficult." Yet despite his all too human failings he has the almost superhuman courage to face the world alone, and a profound conviction that the artist is quasi-divine. This conviction is brought out in one of the most closely written passages in the novel, the description of Stephen after the composition of his villanelle, standing on the steps of the library, ashplant in hand, watching the flight of some birds which he takes to be swallows. After observing the birds minutely, he begins (characteristically) to observe himself observing the birds and to think of himself as an augur in an ancient temple. As overtones of the supernatural increase in intensity, he thinks of his mythical patron, Daedalus, and then, for several moments, of a god who is closely analogous to Stephen.

> A sense of fear of the unknown moved in the heart of his weariness, a fear of symbols and portents, of the hawklike man whose name he bore soaring out of his captivity on osier woven wings, of Thoth, the god of writers, writing with a reed upon a tablet and bearing on his narrow ibis head the cusped moon.
>
> He smiled as he thought of the god's image, for it made him think of a bottlenosed judge in a wig, putting commas into a document which he held at arm's length. . . . [225] [1]

Stephen's mental image of Thoth with a headdress suggesting a judge's wig, the long beak of an ibis, and writing on a tablet held at arm's length closely resembles depictions of the god in the Book of the

From "The Calling of Stephen Dedalus" by Eugene M. Waith, College English, *XVIII (February, 1957), 256–57. Copyright © 1957 by the National Council of Teachers of English. Reprinted by permission of the author and the National Council of Teachers of English.*

[1] See W. Y. Tindall's comment on this passage in his "James Joyce and the Hermetic Tradition," *Journal of the History of Ideas*, XV (1954), 23–39; see also his *The Literary Symbol* (1955), pp. 57–58, 79–84.

Dead at the ceremony of the weighing of the heart. There the deceased is assayed while Thoth, an observer slightly removed, stands ready to add this last judgment to his record of good and evil. Thoth was the scribe of the gods, but he was also much more: he was the god of wisdom, the inventor of speech and letters and, somewhat like the divine *logos*, the one at whose word everything was created. Stephen's "god of writers" is a potent symbol, emblematic in a number of ways of Stephen himself, the artist as a young man, observing, recording, creating.

The suggestion of artistic and divine creativity in this allusion is particularly important as a counterbalance to the suggestion of a satanic fall made most overtly in Stephen's "I will not serve." Two stimulating essays on the *Portrait* have emphasized recently the theme of the fall while neglecting the theme of creativity;[2] the result is a distortion, as it seems to me, of the meaning of the novel. For example, Caroline Gordon believes that one reason for the superiority of this novel to certain others which have a comparable theme "is that Joyce is convinced that his hero is damned." (393) Hugh Kenner, in the course of an excellent demonstration of the structural complexity of the *Portrait*, says, "Ultimately, as the insistent climax of the overture shows, its [the *Portrait's*] central theme is Sin: the development of Stephen Dedalus from a bundle of sensations to a matured, self-conscious, dedicated, fallen being." (142) Though the theme of the fall is undoubtedly significant, it does not occur in isolation, but related and subordinated to what the title of the novel leads us to expect as its main theme, Stephen's development as an artist. The fall is assimilated into the preparations for flight—flight from Ireland and flight on the osier wings of Daedalus, the old artificer to whom Stephen prays in the last words of the novel.

If the central theme is sin, then these final preparations for flight are supremely ironic, and in this way they have been interpreted. After commenting on the "instant of promise" at the end, Kenner goes on to say that in *Ulysses* we see clearly that Stephen's dream of flight is a delusion. He concludes that we should see Stephen, even at the end of *A Portrait*, as an esthete but no artist—a would-be flyer whose fall from grace will soon be followed by another fall like that of Icarus. But there is no indication in *A Portrait* that this kind of irony exists. Ironic detachment there certainly is: no one who has studied the differences between *Stephen Hero* and the final version of the story can doubt that Joyce manipulated the materials of his own life very freely and with great artistic objectivity. He never fails, in

[2] Caroline Gordon, "Some Readings and Misreadings," *Sewanee Review* LXI (1953), 388–393; Hugh Kenner, "The Portrait in Perspective," *James Joyce, Two Decades of Criticism*, ed. Seon Givens (1948) , pp. 132–174.

painting his final portrait, to indicate what is unlikable, weak, or foolish in his adolescent protagonist. Yet to grant all this is not to say that he brands Stephen as already a failure—still less that he shows the failure to be the consequence of rejecting the church. The entire fabric of the novel seems to proclaim its concern with potentialities, with vocation, with the moments leading to the choice of a career. The depiction of this process is brilliantly successful in making the final choice seem the inevitable outgrowth of character. The time has not come for a final judgment and the book makes none, though every stroke of the depiction is informed by a keen moral awareness.

Richard Ellmann

Although Stephen Dedalus in both *Stephen Hero* and *A Portrait* assumes his isolation, he surrounds himself with friends and family to whom he can confide it. When he rebels he hastens to let them know of his rebellion so that he can measure their response to it. He searches for disciples who must share his motives vicariously. As he demands increasing allegiance from them, step by step, he brings them to the point where they will go no further, and their refusal, half-anticipated, enables him to feel forsaken and to forsake them. He buys his own ticket for Holyhead, but claims to have been deported. Yet his mother prepares his clothing for the journey; she at any rate does not break with him. Of this young man it may be safely predicted that he will write letters home.

From "The Growth of Imagination" in James Joyce, *by Richard Ellmann (New York: Oxford University Press, Inc., 1959), p. 302. Copyright © 1959 by Richard Ellmann. Reprinted by permission of Oxford University Press, Inc.*

James Naremore

It is worth observing, as Levin and others have rightly done, that the general characteristics of Joyce's style in the *Portrait* are those of the late Victorians and the decadents: the sensual and violent imagery of Swinburne, the colors of the Pre-Raphaelites, the use of repetition and alliteration, the pervasive air of *Weltschmerz*, and so on. But the use of this paraphernalia is due as much to conscious de-

From "Style as Meaning in A Portrait of the Artist" *by James Naremore,* James Joyce Quarterly, *IV (Summer, 1967), 334–35. Copyright © 1967 by the University of Tulsa. Reprinted by permission of the University of Tulsa and the editor, Thomas F. Staley.*

sign as to unconscious influence; one of the obvious purports of the
book is to suggest the consciousness of a young man who lives at the
turn of the century and who is interested in things literary. It is possible to open the book at almost any page and feel the atmosphere
of literature in the nineties. This passage, for instance:

—A day of dappled seaborne clouds.—

The phrase and the day and the scene harmonised in a chord. Words.
Was it their colours? He allowed them to glow and fade, hue after hue:
sunrise gold, the russet and green of apple orchards, azure of waves, the
greyfringed fleece of clouds. No, it was not their colours: it was the pause
and balance of the period itself. Did he then love the rhythmic rise and
fall of words better than their associations of legend and color? Or was
it that, being as weak of sight as he was shy of mind, he drew less
pleasure from the reflection of the glowing sensible world through the
prism of a language many coloured and richly storied than from the
contemplation of an inner world of individual emotions mirrored perfectly in a lucid supple periodic prose? [166–167]

Atherton, in his edition of the *Portrait*, has traced the phrase "A
day of dappled seaborne clouds" to Hugh Miller's *Testimony of the
Rocks* (Edinburgh, 1869, p. 237).[1] The phrase and the contemplation which follows it may not be an example of "lucid supple periodic
prose," at least not an example of prose in the tradition of Newman,
but it does call to mind Pater and the decadents. Its rich imagery is
even a bit like Keats; and the union of these styles produces something almost like a parody of Hopkins, a poet whom Joyce could not
have known at the time, but a poet with whom both Joyce and
Stephen have affinities.[2] On another level of secondary meaning the
passage catches perfectly the attitudes of the young men of the eighties
and nineties, a new generation disillusioned by the abortive Victorian
attempts to reconcile culture and civilization, a group of artists who
ultimately rejected the "reflection of the glowing sensible world" in
favor of the "contemplation of an inner world of individual emotions."
The notions about aesthetics that are implied by this passage are
pretty clearly out of Pater, just as the pronouncement of an older
Stephen Dedalus at the end of the book, "I go to encounter for the
millionth time the reality of experience and to forge in the smithy of
my soul the uncreated conscience of my race," comes from reading
Yeats and the symbolists.

Joyce's style, then, is carefully designed to give us important information about Stephen Dedalus.

[1] *A Portrait of the Artist* . . . , ed. James S. Atherton (New York, 1963), p. 249.
[2] Anthony Burgess believes that the relation between Joyce's style and Hopkins'
is quite close. See his *ReJoyce* (New York, 1964), pp. 20–21.

Dorothy Van Ghent

One of the oldest themes in the novel is that language is a creator of reality. There is this theme in *Don Quixote*. . . . Quixote is supremely a man animated by "the word"; and as the words he has read in books send him into action—creating reality for him by determining what he sees and what he feels and what he does—so Quixote in turn has a similar effect upon other people, subtly changing their outlook, creating in them new forms of thought and activity. *Don Quixote* may be looked on as an extensive investigation of the creative effects of language upon life. Joyce's *Portrait* is also an investigation of this kind; appropriately so, for the "artist" whose youthful portrait the book is, is at the end to find his vocation in language; and the shape of reality that gradually defines itself for Stephen is a shape determined primarily by the associations of words. We follow in the circumstances of the boy's life the stages of breakdown and increasing confusion in his external environment, as his home goes to pieces, and the correlative stages of breakdown in his inherited values, as his church and his nation lose their authority over his emotions. Very early the child's mind begins to respond to that confusion by seeking in itself, in its own mental images, some unifying form or forms that will signify what the world *really* is, that will show him the *real* logic of things—a logic hopelessly obscure in external relations. His mental images are largely associations suggested by the words he hears, and in intense loneliness he struggles to make the associations fit into a coherent pattern.

To the very young child, adults seem to possess the secret of the whole, seem to know what everything means and how one thing is related to another. Apparently in command of that secret, they toss words together into esoteric compounds, some words whose referents the child knows and many whose referents are mysterious; and the context of the familiar words guides him in his speculation about the unfamiliar ones, the unfamiliar ones thus taking on their meaning for him in a wondrously accidental and chaotic fashion. These accidents of context, however bizarre, build up his notion of reality and determine his later responses and the bias of his soul. There is the story that Stephen's father tells him about a cow coming down along a road. There is the song about the wild rose blossoming on the green place. He, Stephen, is evidently the "nicens little boy" toward whom

From "On A Portrait of the Artist as a Young Man" *in* The English Novel: Form and Function, *by Dorothy Van Ghent, pp. 264–66. Copyright 1953 by Dorothy Van Ghent. Reprinted by permission of Holt, Rinehart and Winston, Inc.*

the cow designs its path, and he, Stephen, can make the wild rose into
a green one by a transposition of adjectives. The world's form, then,
is apparently shaped toward him and out from him as its center. But
how to put the story and the song intelligibly together, in a superior
meaningful pattern of reality, with his father's hairy face looking at
him through a glass? or with the queer smell of the oil sheet? or with
Dante's two brushes? or with Eileen, the neighbor girl, who has a different father and mother? or with some shadowily guilty thing he
has done for which he must "apologize," else eagles will pull out his
eyes? In this extremely short sequence at the beginning of the book,
the child's sense of insecurity, in a world whose form he cannot grasp,
is established—and with insecurity, guilt (he must apologize) and fear
(the horrible eagles). With these unpromising emotional elements
established in him, the maturing child will try again and again to
grasp his world imaginatively as a shape within which he has a part
that is essential to its completeness and harmoniousness and meaningfulness.

Immediately there is a transition to the children's playground
at Clongowes Wood, the child's earliest experience of a community
other than that of the home. Again the auditory impression is pre-
dominant—sounds heard, words spoken—and the life-directed attempt
of the young mind is to understand their meaning in relation to each
other and in relation to a governing design. There are the "strong
cries" of the boys and the "thud" of their feet and bodies; then comes
a quick succession of references to special oddnesses in the names of
things. To the child's laboring apprehension, which assumes all names
to have intimate and honest connections with reality, the name "dog-
in-the-blanket" for the Friday pudding must represent something
about the pudding which is real and which other people know but
which is obscured from him; it may have more than one meaning, like
the word "belt," which means a strap on a jacket and also "to give a
fellow a belt"; or it may have complex, mysterious, and terribly serious
associations with destiny, understood by others but dark and anxious
to himself, like his own name, Stephen Dedalus, which Nasty Roche
says is "queer" with a queerness that puts the social status of Stephen's
father in doubt. Through words the world comes to Stephen; through
the words he hears he gropes his way into other people's images of
reality. Doubts and anxieties arise because the words and phrases are
disassociated, their context frequently arbitrary, like that of the sentences in the spelling book:

> Wolsey died in Leicester Abbey
> Where the abbots buried him.
> Canker is a disease of plants,
> Cancer one of animals. [10]

The sentences in the spelling book at least make a rhythm, and a rhythm is a kind of pattern, a "whole" of sorts; they are therefore "nice sentences" to think about. But the threatening, overwhelming problem is the integration of all the vast heap of disassociated impressions that the child's mind is subjected to and out of which his hopeful urgency toward intelligibility forces him, entirely lonely and without help, to try to make superior rhythms and superior unities.

Ernest Bernhardt-Kabisch

—Stephanos Dedalos! Bous Stephanoumenos! Bous Stephaneforos!

This strange, quasi-Greek line occurs at so crucial a moment in Joyce's novel (168) that one wonders why it has been so generally ignored. To all appearances mere banter and gibberish, it contains in fact the gist of the whole book, expressing the "prophecy of the end [Stephen] had been born to serve" (169) in a series of richly allusive leitmotifs.

The first motif, "Stephanos Dedalos," requires little explanation. As Stephen himself feels, his "strange name," made more strange and portentous by the Grecizing form, now signifies not merely an alternative but a direction: it becomes a "prophecy" of Stephen's imminent conversion from the priesthood of religion, represented by St. Stephen, to the priesthood of art, whose archetype is Daedalus, the "Cunning Artificer."

The remaining two motifs, while continuing to pun on the hero's name, suggest a somewhat different complex of ideas. *Bous* is the Greek word for bull, bullock, ox, etc. *Stephanoumenos* means "being crowned," "wreathed," or "garlanded" for various occasions, notably for sacrifice (*stephanoumenos tō theō,* "being wreathed for the god"). The bull, of course, as Sir James Frazer and others have shown, is conspicuous in mythology not only as a symbol of strength and fertility, but as the epiphany of various year gods and vegetation divinities, notably Dionysus and Osiris, and as such figures frequently as sacrificial victim in the mysteries commemorating the death of the god. In ancient bull-worshipping Crete of Daedalean fame bulls were killed, torn to pieces, and devoured to commemorate the death and laceration of Dionysus and to re-enact the sacramental eating of the flesh and drinking of the blood of the killed god. The bull was likewise the victim in the Roman Attis cult. This bull was decorated with garlands

From "Joyce's A Portrait of the Artist as a Young Man" *by Ernest Bernhardt-Kabisch, The Explicator, XVIII (January, 1960), article no. 24. Copyright © 1960 by The Explicator. Reprinted by permission of the author and The Explicator. Professor Bernhardt-Kabisch has made minor revisions in his original article.*

of flowers, and his horns were woven round with a wreath of golden leaves. His blood was believed to wash away the initiate's sins. "Bous stephanoumenos" thus clearly connotes "sacrifice and death."

Now if *stephanoumenos* can mean "designated for sacrifice," *stephane-phoros*, "wreath-bearing," never does, but is always an epithet of honor applied to high public officials in the Greek *polis*, notably to priests (*Phoibou stephanephoros hiereus*, "wreath-bearing priest of Phoebus"). "Bous stephaneforos," then, is the bull not as victim but as victor, epiphany of the god risen from death, exalted, and glorified, shaking off the fetters of earth to attain full apotheosis.

Thus the incantation sums up not only Stephen's passing from the proposed priesthood of the Christian religion to the chosen priesthood of the "Dedalean" creed, but the whole of his Dionysian passion, death, and resurrection. At a later point, Stephen thinks of himself as "a priest of eternal imagination, transmuting the daily bread of experience into the radiant body of everliving life" (221): here the sacramental killing and eating of the god ("Bous stephanoumenos") has been transformed into the eucharist itself. He wants "to live, to err, to fall, to triumph, to recreate life out of life," to pass along "all the ways of error and glory" (172)—to be, that is, a pagan and therefore more human Christ, who not only lives, falls, and triumphs, but who also errs as men do. "Stephaneforos! . . . His soul had arisen from the grave of boyhood, spurning her graveclothes" (169–170): now the bull has disappeared, the god reveals himself in his true essence, as *Daidalos Dionysos*.

Standing there on the shore of North Bull Island (!), proud and ecstatic, Stephen is at once the giver, the receiver, and the victim of a religious sacrifice, at once priest, god, and martyr of his new Dedalean religion of Art.

Florence L. Walzl

What Joyce meant by the term *epiphany* may be deduced etymologically. The basic meaning in Greek of ἐπιφάνεια is *appearance* or *manifestation*, and the word is related to a verb meaning *to display* or *show forth* and in the passive and middle voice *to shine forth*. In the early Christian period *epiphaneia* developed a religious denotation as a "visible manifestation of a hidden divinity either in the form of a

From "The Liturgy of the Epiphany Season and the Epiphanies of Joyce" by Florence L. Walzl, PMLA, *LXXX (1965), 436–37. Copyright © 1965 by the Modern Language Association of America. Reprinted by permission of the Modern Language Association of America. Some of the footnotes have been deleted with the permission of the publisher. Those retained have been renumbered.*

personal appearance, or by some deed of power by which its presence is made known." [1] It also refers specifically to the feast of the Epiphany, 6 January.

That Joyce used the word in both the general and restricted senses seems indicated in *Stephen Hero*, where Stephen discusses the epiphanies he is writing and relates them to his esthetic theory. This theory developed in part from his linguistic interests, in that his concern with words as symbols [*SH*, 26–27] led to a concern with reproducing both the reality of an event and its symbolic or spiritual meaning. Joyce describes how a commonplace incident which seemed a symbol of "Irish paralysis" made Stephen "think of collecting many such moments together in a book of epiphanies." [*SH*, 211] "By an epiphany," Joyce continues, Stephen "meant a sudden spiritual manifestation, whether in the vulgarity of speech or of gesture or in a memorable phase of the mind itself. He believed that it was for the man of letters to record these epiphanies with extreme care, seeing that they themselves are the most delicate and evanescent of moments." This definition adopts the basic Greek meaning of *manifestation* but reflects the later sense of the word as a revelation of inner significance by means of outward appearance. When Joyce goes on to relate his epiphany to his threefold concept of art as "wholeness, symmetry and radiance," the idea of "shining forth" is also apparent: the moment an object is viewed in perspective by an artist, its "soul" leaps from its "appearance," it becomes "radiant," and is thus "epiphanised." [*SH*, 210–213] The beholder's realization of this manifestation of identity is like a flash of intellectual light. Joyce's concept of epiphany appears also to be colored by the popular association of the feast of the Epiphany with the star which symbolized the spiritual illumination that led the Magi to the Christ child. Joyce's early view of the epiphany is exemplified in the twenty-two prose epiphanies dating from this period. All bare paragraphs of less than 150 words, they recreate "evanescent . . . moments"; however, since they are entirely without a frame of reference, most seem trivial or meaningless. (It is significant that when Joyce adapted some of them for his mature fiction, he fitted them into a chronological framework.) Joyce's epiphanies have largely been explained on the basis of this background.

The term *epiphany* is often applied to the *Dubliners* stories. Yet it is not always noted that when Joyce planned the collection he called the pieces *epicleti*. What did he mean by this term and how did he derive it? It first appears in a comment he made on the stories for *The Irish Homestead*: "I am writing a series of epicleti—ten—for a paper. . . . I call the series *Dubliners* to betray the soul of that hemiplegia or paralysis which many consider a city." [2] This term seems

---

[1] William F. Arndt and F. Wilbur Gingrich, *A Greek-English Lexicon of the New Testament and Other Early Christian Literature* (Chicago, 1957).

[2] James Joyce, *Letters*, ed. Stuart Gilbert (New York, 1957), p. 55.

either an adaptation of or a mistake for epiclesis (or epiklesis),[3] and an invented plural. The epiklesis is an invocation of the ancient Mass liturgies which besought God the Father through the Holy Spirit to transform the bread and wine into the body and blood of Jesus. The epiklesis has virtually disappeared from Western liturgy, but the Eastern Church regards it as the "essential form of the sacrament," the act effecting the transubstantiation in the Mass.[4] (It is equivalent in the Latin rite to the Words of Institution which repeat Jesus' statements at the Last Supper and represent the most solemn moment of the Mass.) Joyce's adoption of this term indicates that he believed the artist's creative act was analogous to the eucharistic change effected by the priest. Such a view is supported by Joyce's application of priest-like names to the artist in *Stephen Hero* ("penitent," "confessor," and "mediator"; [*SH*, 32, 77, 202–203] by his later description of Stephen in the *Portrait* as "a priest of eternal imagination, transmuting the daily bread of experience into the radiant body of everliving life"; [221] and by a conversation reported by Joyce's brother in which Joyce spoke of a resemblance between his work and the Mass, in that he aimed to give an "intellectual pleasure or spiritual enjoyment by converting the bread of everyday life into something that has a permanent artistic life." [5] The term *epicleti* thus refers to the artist's eucharist.

Though *epicleti* and *epiphanies* are related words, they are not synonyms. The epicleti are the creative processes; the epiphanies, the resulting manifestations. Such a distinction had its probable origin in the Mass: just as the priest first effects the transubstantiation, uniting himself in communion with Divinity, and only later in distributing communion affords the laity a similar experience, so in Joyce's view the writer transforms real experience into art, having in the process godlike insights into the nature of things, as a result of which his work of art later offers a like experience to the reader.

Irene Hendry Chayes

In the *Portrait*, which covers in 93 pages events that require 234 pages in the *Hero* fragment, the original elements of Joyce's first novel, particularly the characters, are subjected to a process of compression and distillation that rejects all irrelevancies, all particularities and ambiguities, and leaves only their pure essence. In *Stephen Hero*, the

From "Joyce's Epiphanies" by Irene Hendry Chayes, Sewanee Review, LIV (July, 1946), 158–59. Copyright 1946 by the University of the South. Reprinted by permission of the University of the South.

[3] Ibid., and Ellmann, p. 169.
[4] Adrian Fortescue, "Epiklesis," *The Catholic Encyclopedia*, 1909, v, 502–503.
[5] *My Brother's Keeper*, pp. 103–104. See Ellmann, p. 169.

common people at the Good Friday service are diverse in their sub-
missive ignorance and their unquestioning respect for the clergy; the
old women scrape their hands over the dry bottom of the holy-water
font and speak in broad, realistic dialect. But in the *Portrait* the
simple faithful are represented by pious sighs and a peasant smell "of
air and rain and turf and corduroy," [18] or by kneeling forms and
whispering voices in the confessional box—"soft whispering cloudlets,
soft whispering vapour, whispering and vanishing." [142] In the first
draft of the novel, Maurice and Isabel Dedalus appear specifically as
characters; in the *Portrait*, Stephen's brothers and sisters are merely
voices at the tea-table, replying to his questions in pig-latin or singing
with an "overtone of weariness behind their frail fresh innocent
voices." [163] "He heard the choir of voices in the kitchen echoed and
multiplied through an endless reverberation of the choirs of endless
generations of children: and heard in all the echoes an echo also of
the recurring note of weariness and pain. All seemed weary of life
even before entering upon it." [164]

The character of Stephen itself undergoes a transformation. The
Hero draft is often marred by adolescent particularities: Stephen bait-
ing his cruder classmates, sneering at his mother's pious superstitions,
or trying to convert his parents to Ibsen. In the *Portrait*, however,
the Ibsen episode is omitted entirely, the intellectual distance between
Stephen and his contemporaries is given less emphasis, and the quarrel
with his mother over his failure to do his Easter duty is mentioned
only indirectly. The details of Stephen's debauches similarly remain
obscure; what we are shown, in the boy's dreams of temptation, the
sermons he listens to during the retreat, and his hallucinations of
damnation and punishment, is actually an apotheosis—or epiphany—
of sin and repentance, far removed from the adventures of the Eugene
Gants who for a generation have been storming the brothels of the
world in imitation of Stephen.

But the most striking attenuation occurs in the character of Emma
Clery. In the *Hero* fragment, she is a healthy, middle-class girl who
studies Gaelic with enthusiasm, flirts with priests, and is only confused
and offended by Stephen's unconventional offer of himself. In the
Portrait, however, we are told nothing of her appearance and are
never allowed a clear conception of her as an individual. The Gaelic
lessons shrink to an Irish phrase-book, the flirtation becomes a bitter
recollection in Stephen's mind, associated with the scorn he feels for
the Church, and there is only the barest hint of the circumstances of
the rejection. The girl herself is never more than a shadowy presence—
a provocative glance or speech, a shawled head, "fresh warm breath,"
laughter and tapping footsteps, a sash or a nodding hair ornament.
Her etherealization extends even to her name, which in the *Portrait*
becomes "E—— C——."

Chronology of Important Dates

	Joyce	The Age
1882	James Joyce born on February 2 in Rathgar, a suburb of Dublin.	
1888–91	Attended Clongowes Wood College at Clane.	
1891		Death of Charles Stewart Parnell.
1893–98	Attended Belvedere College, Dublin.	
1898–1902	Attended University College, Dublin.	
1899		Yeats' *Countess Cathleen* produced in Dublin. Boer War began.
1902–1903	Lived in Paris.	
1904	Wrote "A Portrait of the Artist" (sketch); began *Stephen Hero;* and left for the Continent with Nora Barnacle.	Bloomsday (*Ulysses*), June 16. Opening of the Abbey Theatre.
1905		Russo-Japanese War.
1907	*Chamber Music* published; *Stephen Hero* abandoned; the *Portrait* begun.	
1914–15	*Dubliners* published in London; the *Portrait* published serially in *The Egoist,* London. *Ulysses* begun.	World War I began.
1915	Wrote *Exiles.*	
1916	The *Portrait* published in New York.	Easter Rebellion in Ireland.
1919		Treaty of Versailles.
1922	*Ulysses* published in Paris.	Irish Free State established.
1929		Stock Market Crash.

	Joyce	*The Age*
1933	Judge John M. Woolsey ruled *Ulysses* not pornographic.	Hitler appointed Chancellor of Germany. Roosevelt inaugurated President of the United States.
1934	*Ulysses* published in New York.	
1939	*Finnegans Wake* published.	World War II began.
1941	Died on January 13, Zürich.	

Notes on the Editor and Contributors

WILLIAM M. SCHUTTE, the editor, is Lucia R. Briggs Professor of English at Lawrence University. He is the author of *Joyce and Shakespeare*.

ERNEST BERNHARDT-KABISCH is Associate Professor of English at Indiana University.

IRENE HENDRY CHAYES, who teaches at the State University of New York at Binghamton, has written on the English Romantic Poets.

WAYNE BOOTH, author of *The Rhetoric of Fiction,* is George M. Pullman Professor of English at the University of Chicago.

RICHARD ELLMANN has written biographies of both Joyce and Yeats and a critical study of the latter. He is Franklin Bliss Snyder Professor of English at Northwestern University.

S. L. GOLDBERG, Robert Wallace Professor of English at the University of Melbourne, has published two extended studies of Joyce.

HUGH KENNER has written books on Joyce, Pound, Wyndham Lewis, and Beckett. His essay "The Portrait in Perspective" opened a new era in Joyce criticism. He is now Professor of English at the University of California, Santa Barbara.

LEE T. LEMON, Associate Professor of English at the University of Nebraska, is associate editor of *Prairie Schooner* and author of books and articles about literary criticism.

HARRY LEVIN wrote a pioneer study of Joyce in 1941, edited *The Portable James Joyce,* and has written several other books of criticism. He is the Irving Babbitt Professor of Comparative Literature at Harvard University.

JAMES NAREMORE is an instructor in English at the University of Wisconsin.

JOSEPH PRESCOTT, Professor of English at Wayne State University, has written many articles on Joyce. The article which appears in this volume has been widely reprinted and translated into at least six languages.

BARBARA SEWARD, who died in 1958, was author of *The Symbolic Rose* and articles on modern fiction.

F. PARVIN SHARPLESS, who has published a book on John Stuart Mill, is Head of the Department of English at Germantown Friends School in Philadelphia.

J. I. M. STEWART, literary critic, novelist, and writer of detective fiction, has been a Student of Christ Church, Oxford, since 1949.

DOROTHY VAN GHENT is the author of *The English Novel: Form and Function*.

EUGENE M. WAITH, Professor of English at Yale University, has written extensively on Tudor and Stuart Drama.

FLORENCE L. WALZL is Professor of English at the University of Wisconsin, Milwaukee. She has written several articles on Joyce.

Selected Bibliography

On Joyce

Ellmann, Richard. *James Joyce*. New York: Oxford University Press, 1959. The standard biography.

Goldberg, S. L. *James Joyce*. New York: Grove Press, 1962. An excellent brief introduction to Joyce's work by a critic who believes that *Ulysses* is his masterpiece and *Finnegans Wake* not worth detailed exegesis.

Kenner, Hugh. *Dublin's Joyce*. Bloomington: Indiana University Press, 1956. A difficult, provocative critical study.

Magalaner, Marvin, and Kain, Richard M. *Joyce: The Man, The Work, The Reputation*. New York: New York University Press, 1956. An extended, loosely organized survey of biographical problems, the initial reception of the individual works, and Joyce's critical reputation. The authors also attempt to solve selected critical problems posed by each work.

Noon, William T. *Joyce and Aquinas*. New Haven: Yale University Press, 1957. A difficult but rewarding study which throws light on the aesthetic theory of Stephen Dedalus.

Sullivan, Kevin. *Joyce Among the Jesuits*. New York: Columbia University Press, 1958. Contains much useful information about Joyce's school and university experiences.

On The Portrait

(NOTE: Articles included in the Anderson, Connolly, and Morris-Nault collections have not been listed separately.)

Anderson, Chester G. *A Portrait of the Artist as a Young Man: Text, Criticism, and Notes*. New York: The Viking Press, 1968. The text is that of the 1964 Viking Compass edition with the pagination unchanged. The seventy pages of notes are accurate and helpful. Also included are related texts by Joyce (including "A Portrait of the Artist"), early commentary, and ten critical essays.

Brandabur, Edward. "Stephen's Aesthetic in *A Portrait of the Artist*," in *The Celtic Cross*, ed. Ray B. Browne, *et al*. Lafayette, Indiana: Purdue

University Press, 1964. Demonstrates that the real significance of Stephen's aesthetic theory depends on its dramatic context.

Connolly, Thomas E., ed. *Joyce's Portrait: Criticisms and Critiques.* New York: Appleton-Century-Crofts, 1962. Contains selections devoted to various aspects of the *Portrait* and a section of eight essays on Stephen's aesthetic theory.

Hancock, Leslie. *Word Index to James Joyce's Portrait of the Artist.* Carbondale and Edwardsville: Southern Illinois University Press, 1967. Prepared with the assistance of a computer, this is a helpful tool for studying the language of the *Portrait* and for locating elusive passages.

Manso, Peter. "The Metaphoric Style of Joyce's *Portrait.*" *Modern Fiction Studies,* XIII (Summer 1967), 221–236. Chiefly useful for its analysis of Joyce's views about style.

Morris, William E., and Nault, Clifford A., Jr., eds. *Portraits of the Artist: A Casebook on James Joyce's A Portrait of the Artist as a Young Man.* New York: The Odyssey Press, Inc., 1962. A wide-ranging selection of essays on the *Portrait.* Many are important, some of dubious value.

Scholes, Robert E. "Stephen Dedalus: *Eiron* and *Alazon.*" *Texas Studies in Language and Literature,* III (Spring 1961), 8–15. A useful contribution to the debate on aesthetic distance. Scholes concludes that Joyce intended Stephen to be both *eiron* and *alazon.*

————, and Kain, Richard M. *The Workshop of Daedalus: James Joyce and the Raw Materials for A Portrait of the Artist as a Young Man.* Evanston: Northwestern University Press, 1965. A gathering of personal and general materials relevant to Joyce's achievement in the *Portrait.*

Thrane, James R. "Joyce's Sermon on Hell: Its Sources and Its Backgrounds." *Modern Philology,* LVII (February 1960), 172–198. Analyzes Joyce's extensive use of Father Giovanni Pietro Pinamonti's *Hell Opened to Christians* in composing the two retreat sermons on Hell.